To Peter & Ei

Anecdotes
of the
Anglo-Boer War

Rob Milne

With best wishes from

Rob Milne

Anecdotes
of the
Anglo-Boer War
Rob Milne

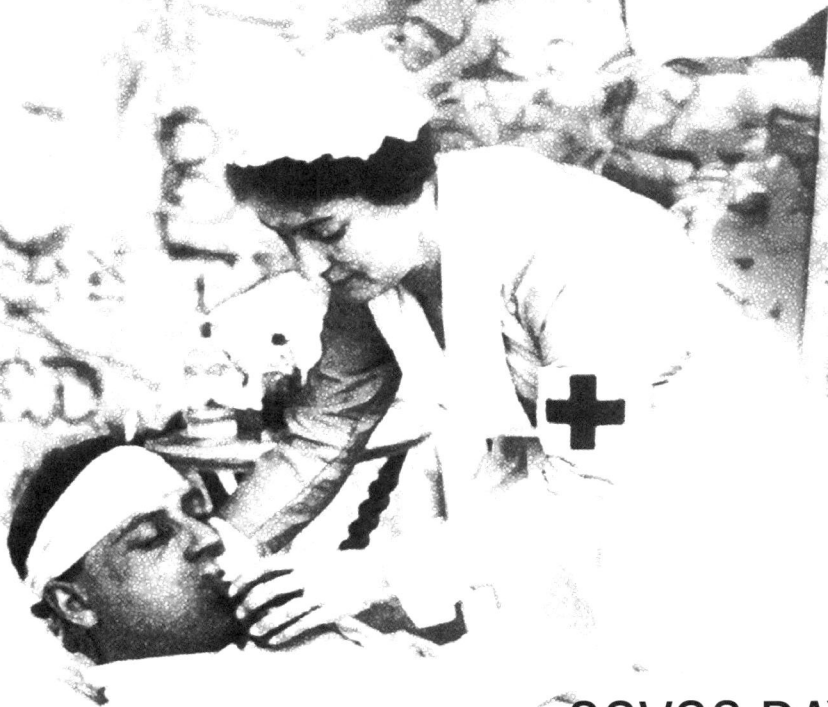

COVOS DAY

Published by Covos Day Books, 2000
Oak Tree House, Tamarisk Avenue,
P.O. Box 6996, Weltevredenpark 1715, South Africa

Copyright © Rob Milne 2000

Cover Design by JANT Design
Design and origination by JANT Design
+27 12 664-2241, email: j.design@mweb.co.za

Map by Genevieve Edwards

Printed and bound by United Litho

ISBN 0-620-25439-4

Dedicated
to
my mother and father
Margaret and Stanley Milne

Author's Note and Acknowledgments

This is a book about the people who fought in the Anglo-Boer War and how it has touched many lives, even up to the present. It has its origins in stories swapped around campfires, dinner tables and during battlefield explorations. In trying to make sense of this, the "last of the gentlemen's wars", I have met many people whose input, encouragement, and friendship I value deeply. These are people from all walks of life and whose roots stem from both sides of the conflict, some of whom I know only as a voice on the telephone or through an email.

So many names come to mind, and I apologize if I have omitted anyone. Thanks to my family for helping me with much of the field-work, David Panagos (who gave me valuable input in the field and advice on my first manuscript), Les Faber, Beth Strachan, Brian Khaigan, Diana Maddon and the staff of the Brenthust Library, Jane Theron, Huffy and Cherry Pott, Jean Beater of the National Monuments Council, Morris Gough-Palmer, Roger and Debby Webster, Betty de Lange and the staff of the SA Museum of Military History Library, Bekky Smit, Alistair and Marion Moir, Gerda Whitehorn, Desmarie Coetzee, Tig Warne, Jack Seale, Muriel Bates, Patricia Glyn, Shirley Stone, Raymond and Margaret West, Professor Louis Changuion, John and Jean Reid, Dana van Vuuren, Slava Kustanovich, Rensie van Rensburg, Muriel Falconer, Flo Bird, Den Adams, Jasmine and Ferdie Coetzee, Lyn Miller, Appels and Sarie Appelcryn. A special thank you to Martyn Day and Lyn Voigt for editing the book, and Chris Cocks for publishing it.

I have quoted extensively from published sources and have made every effort to trace the copyright holders. Should any infringements have inadvertently occurred, I apologize and undertake to correct any omissions in future editions.

Rob Milne
Hennops River, 2000

Foreword

Rob Milne inspired many enthusiasts with his particular approach to history when he first appeared on my radio programme "Patricia's People" (SAfm 104 – 107) back in February 1999. I think that, like me, listeners loved his small brush strokes on the large canvas of our past, his interest in the intimate stories of love, loyalty, pettiness and cruelty that characterized this (and indeed any) human conflict. Most accounts of this dramatic period concentrate on politics, tactics, firepower and logistics and I believe that many of these tales would have been lost to our archives but for Rob's relentless ferreting in koppie and dorp around South Africa. I congratulate him on the passion with which he has pursued this interest and am delighted that these precious stories are now in print.

Patricia Glyn

N

Tropic of Capricorn

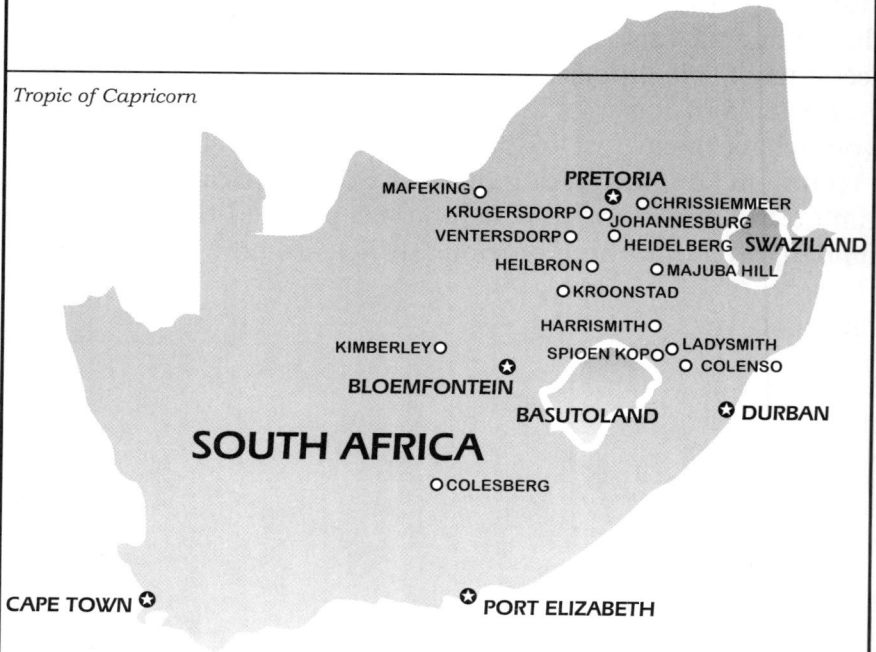

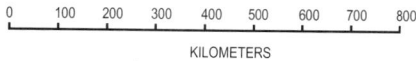

MAFEKING O

PRETORIA ✪
O CHRISSIEMMEER
KRUGERSDORP O O O JOHANNESBURG
VENTERSDORP O O HEIDELBERG SWAZILAND
HEILBRON O O MAJUBA HILL
O KROONSTAD
HARRISMITH O
KIMBERLEY O SPIOEN KOPO O O LADYSMITH
✪ O COLENSO
BLOEMFONTEIN
BASUTOLAND ✪ DURBAN

SOUTH AFRICA

O COLESBERG

CAPE TOWN ✪   ✪ PORT ELIZABETH

0   100   200   300   400   500   600   700   800

KILOMETERS

SOUTH AFRICA

CONTENTS

A

A perspective

This book is mainly concerned with the Second Anglo-Boer War, although I do sometimes touch on other events between the First Anglo-Boer War and the Second World War. Herman Charles Bosman, the famous South African short story writer, gave this perspective on the difference between the First and Second Anglo-Boer Wars: "Exciting times followed. There was a great deal of shooting at the leopard and a great deal of running away from him. The amount of Martini and Mauser fire I heard in the

A centenary tribute by Afrikaans schoolchildren in the British military cemetery at Sannah's Post (Koorn Spruit) near Bloemfontein. The children's names are written on the pebbles, with their touching messages of reconciliation.

The comments in the visitors' book in the small museum recall Kitchener's words to the Boer delegates after the signing of the Peace Treaty at the end of the War, "We are all friends now". These comments are repeated by both English and Afrikaans- speaking South African visitors.

krantzes reminded me of nothing so much as the First Boer War. And the amount of running away reminded me of nothing so much as the Second Boer War". (Bosman, 1964, p.29).

I should immediately say that I give this anecdote as a humorous introduction and not as a depreciation of the Boer efforts, for I have nothing but admiration for the two small Boer Republics, which held out against the might of the British Empire for three years. Bosman laughs at his people and himself, and indeed you will find in this collection that, apart from stories about the crazy antics of the British generals, the Boers themselves initiated many of the humorous exchanges that took place during the war.

A Scout dies

Danie Theron, who formed and led the Boer Scouting Corps, died alone in a barrage of British artillery fire on a ridge near Fochville. What drove him to such recklessness that he single-handedly engaged a whole British column? The answer goes back to 1893, when he set up a successful legal practice in Krugersdorp and met a young woman called Johanna Neethling whom he intended to marry. Every weekend he cycled from

Danie Theron's memorial near Fochville, on the ridge where he died alone in a barrage of British artillery fire.

Krugersdorp to Eikenhof and back, a distance of 26 miles, to be with her. In August 1898 she caught a chill, which developed into pneumonia, and she died on the 28th, in the same bed and on the same day as her sister, Henrietta. "There can be little doubt that her death was a great blow to Theron, who never married". (DSAB vol. 2, 1972, p.738). It was just eight days after the second anniversary of her death, on 5th September 1900, that Theron came to grief in his final act of defiant recklessness. His comrades, aware of the tragic motivation for his reckless bravery, arranged for his reburial after the war. Danie Theron now rests in peace beside his beloved Joanna in the small cemetery at Eikenhof.

Danie Theron's final resting place next to his beloved Johanna who is buried with her sister in the grave to the right of Danie's with the elaborate headstone.

A shot in the head

The high-powered Boer Mauser rifles inflicted clean wounds with their flat trajectories, and there are numerous reports of British soldiers recovering from chest wounds after just a few days' convalescence. In some cases the Mauser bullet improved performance. "Captain Dibley was almost on top of the hill [Talana] when hit. He had a dim recollection of the gallant adjutant of the Royal Irish Fusiliers racing up almost alongside him and within a few paces of the summit, when he suddenly saw an aged and gray-bearded burgher drawing a bead upon him at a distance of a few paces only. He snapped his revolver at the burgher, only to fall senseless next moment with a bullet through his head. Marvellous though it seems he made a comparatively speedy recovery, and was able to ride into Ladysmith, at the head of his company the following February, having been in the hospital in the besieged town in the interval. Evidence of the temporary nature of the discomfort caused by a bullet through the head is afforded by the fact that he is today one of the best bridge players in the Regiment". (Romer, 1908, pp.11 – 12).

On 4th June 1901, Lord Methuen's column was attacked as it was leaving Jacobsdal. "On our side Lieutenant King, of the General's escort, was shot through the brain and two others were also wounded. Though Lieutenant King's brains actually protruded from the wound, he eventually recovered". (Guest, 1902, p.91).

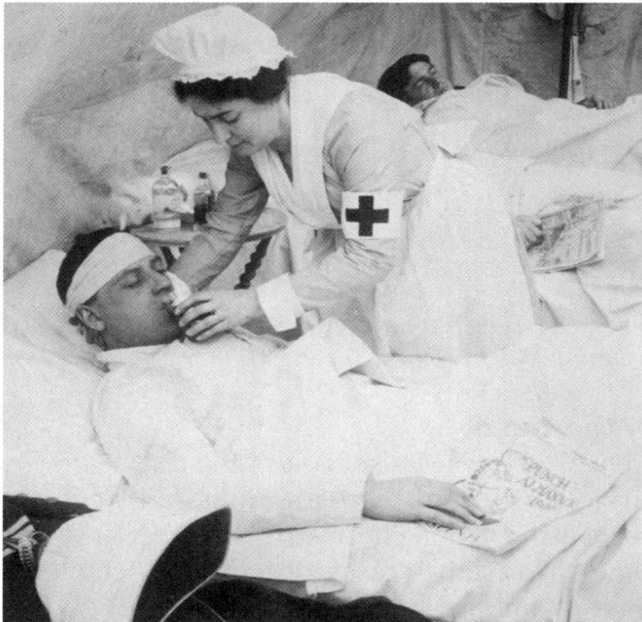

In a Field Hospital on the Tugela River.

Advancing with the enemy

During the attack on the British camp at Lake Chrissie, a Canadian Scout sent by General French with a dispatch to General Smith-Dorrien, arrived at 3 am and found himself in the midst of the Boers who were about to commence their attack. He lay low and as the Boers advanced he followed and ended up in the camp where he delivered the message and, "… saluting, handed me the dispatch with as much unconcern as though it had been an Aldershot field day". At one stage during the advance he noticed a Boer looking at him with some interest, so he pushed the muzzle of his carbine into the Boer's back and pulled the trigger, reasoning that "dead men tell no tales". (Smith-Dorrien, 1925, pp.276 – 277).

Alcohol

General Buller had to have a constant supply of champagne to sustain him in the field, which goes a long way to explain his often-irrational decisions. At one time he was anxiously awaiting an order of 50 cases of champagne from his wine merchant in England, to whom he had given the strictest instructions to label the consignment "castor oil". In reply to an inquiring signal to his military base, an officer replied: "Regret exceedingly no cases as described have yet reached us, but this day we have procured all the castor oil possible (20 cases), and have dispatched it without delay, as you desired. We trust this unavoidable delay has caused no serious inconvenience". (Griffith, 1974, p.318).

After General Viljoen's successful attack on the British forts at Helvetia, the British prisoners filled their water bottles with rum looted from their own stores. As they were being marched back to the Boer camp near Dullstroom, Schikkerling watched a prisoner riding on one of the Boers' horses, periodically handing his water bottle down to his meek captor. "The latter once more looked up appealingly and the prisoner said 'No more left.' The captor's meek and appealing attitude now suddenly changed and he shouted: 'Then get off that bloody horse!'" (Schikkerling, 1964, p.119).

Jack van den Heever and his brother, Gert, lay exposed for many hours in the hot sun near Val station, waiting to blow up a goods train. Their expectations were not in vain, as the train that was disabled contained "fat plunder", and was afterwards known as the "whisky train". Jack was so thirsty from exposure that he drained many bottles of different types of alcohol, and afterwards had to be taken back to camp on the back of a mule cart. (Uys, 1981, p.96).

Words of wisdom written in 1963 by my great-uncle, a gunner who served with the Royal Field Artillery during the Anglo-Boer War: "Alcohol is a good friend but a bad master".

Ammunition
It became regular practice for the Boer commandos to follow British columns to replenish their ammunition. The British would not trouble to pick up cartridges that fell from their bandoliers and that could be easily replaced at camp. Reitz commented: '… I doubt if the British ever realized to what an extent the Boers were dependent upon this source of replenishment.' (Reitz, 1929, pp.187 – 188). Even today, a century after the war, it is surprising how many unfired cartridges can be found in the veld.

An American dies
On 15th July 1901, an Irish American called Walter Wilson, fighting on the side of the Boers, was badly wounded in a skirmish. The British allowed Chris, his countryman and messmate, onto the battlefield to hear his dying words. Wilson said: 'Say good-bye to the boys, and tell them we will meet at the Great Divide.' (Schikkerling, 1964, pp.256 – 257).

An angel smiles
There simply has to be an interesting story behind the two graves of Sergeant Woodward in the Kloof cemetery, Heidelberg. On his cast-iron cross his date of death is recorded as 8th August 1900, and his engraved stone memorial is two graves away. The story is told in the papers of the late Jurie Swart who recorded it on

20th January 1949, from the evidence of two witnesses, a priest and a local woman.

Sergeant Woodward's two graves in the Kloof cemetery, Heidelberg. The one on the left of the memorial in the foreground has a cast-iron cross, whist the one on the right has a headstone.

Woodward was sent on a dangerous mission, but never returned. Some time later an English unit came across his skeleton on the veld and identified him from some papers, which were still legible. His remains were brought to Heidelberg and he received a funeral with full military honours. Meantime, a different reconnaissance group had been interviewing farm workers and Boer prisoners of war in another area, and heard another account of his death. Farm labourers reported that they had seen two Boers bludgeon Woodward to death with an axe and a pick handle, and they had then seen them burying his remains on a hill. Some time later, Woodward's remains were recovered from the hill and he was again buried with full military honours by the new British garrison, who had no idea of his earlier burial. Having been a bagpipe player of note, he was dressed in full Scottish uniform, bagpipe and all, so that he would be fully equipped for the Resurrection. It was a very emotional funeral, what with the bagpipes playing and the women weeping.

Many years later it was rumoured that the second set of Woodward's remains was actually that of a Suikerbosrand farmer's pet baboon, who killed it before he fled from the advancing British Army. Someone asked the priest: 'And what will happen on the Final Day when, amid trumpet calls, the baboon appears among the English soldiers?' The embarrassed priest answered: 'What they will do to the baboon I don't know, but this I know full well—if he appears in the company of English soldiers in full Scottish regalia with bagpipes under his arm, even the Angel in charge won't be able to suppress a smile.'

An atrocity

After the armoured train was captured near Chieveley, a rumour went around that the Boers had buried one of the Dublins alive. Next to the mass grave is a solitary grave in memory of an Unknown Soldier. "A poor fellow of the Dublins had his leg shot off, and it is supposed he crawled away, and the Boers buried him alive, for afterwards he was found with his other leg out of the ground. And when we dug up his body he was found to be clutching the ground with both hands. Our doctor said he could not have lived, and the Boers doubtless thought him dead, so we don't blame them for it". (Griffith, 1974, p.155).

Aerial warfare

The Royal Engineers arrived in South Africa with 20 balloons, which proved to be largely ineffectual owing to the fact that they were graded for a height of 4,000 feet at Aldershot, at sea level. Ladysmith, for example, is at an altitude of 3,500 feet and so the balloons could go no higher than 500 feet. The balloons were heavy, because the fabric was made from rubberized sailcloth. The journalist J. B. Atkins commented: 'I hope the aeronauts will manage to get it up by relieving it of the cradle and sending up some light, acrobatic observer in the ropes. Otherwise I fear that when we get to a still higher place in the hills the balloon will try to go through the ground!' (Coetzer, 1996, p.107). His observation was quite shrewd as the Transvaal highveld has an altitude of 6,000 feet.

Balloon Corps transport with Lord Roberts's advance on Johannesburg.

During the Siege of Ladysmith the Royal Engineers operated a total of eight observation balloons. The balloons were khaki in colour, each balloon being filled with 11,000 cubic feet of gas. The attached wicker basket carried two men. The balloons were fixed to the ground with ropes and communication was via a telephone link. The Boers realized that it was futile to try to shoot them down with artillery when they were in the air, so they worked out the exact launch position, and shelled them when they descended. (Bella Crow). By the fourth day of the siege two balloons had been lost by shellfire, and one in a storm.

During the Battle of Magersfontein a war balloon was kept in the air for most of the day but directed the naval gun to shoot over the back of the hill instead of shelling the Boer trenches. "... to the present-day the ground at the rear of the hill is strewn thickly

with the bones of hundreds of horses, the effect of the naval pills".
(Guest, 1902, p.48).

A Boer officer, Captain J.J. Naude, gave an interesting explanation for the British defeat at Nicholson's Nek. Prior to the British attack they had observed the Boer positions from a war balloon, but the Boers had purposely deployed their forces very thinly in the centre. After the balloon came down, the evening before the early morning attack, Joubert re-deployed forces into the centre, thus beating the British back in a near rout. (Scholtz, 1940, p.21).

Baron H. von Zeppelin (leader of the Hollander Volunteer Contingent), who died of wounds received at Elandslaagte, was a relation of the German airship designer. After the war he was re-buried in the Kloof cemetery, Heidelberg. (Uys, 1981, p.9).

Headstone of Baron H. von Zeppelin in the Kloof cemetery, Heidelberg.

Attraction

Whilst on commando in September 1901, Schikkerling was attracted to a young lady of about 18. 'In the religion of love, I have, in these peaceful days, reason to believe that I am not entirely an atheist.' (Schikkerling, 1964, p.308).

B

Baggage

Lieutenant Fuller's field kit was not supposed to exceed 50 pounds and he was a little surprised to discover that he had no fewer than 14 different boxes and bundles. However, he observed that he was not as bad as his colonel, who carried with him a one-roomed corrugated iron house "...for this was a gentleman's war". (Fuller, 1937, pp.134 to 135).

Lord Basing's cavalry column, the Royals, did itself proud as each officer had his own Cape cart. "When this column halted and outspanned near the Bothaville drift, what with the cracking of whips, the yells of the voorloopers, the smoke of the fires, the galloping of horses and the erection of tents, the scene must have

Corrugated iron buildings in Belfast, erected by the British Army during the Anglo Boer War.

closely resembled the Israelites entering the Holy Land. I have never witnessed anything quite so immobile in my life". (Fuller, 1937, p.243).

Winston Churchill observed: 'The vast amount of baggage this army takes with it on the march hampers its movements and utterly precludes all possibility of surprising the enemy.' And also: 'It is a poor economy to let a soldier live well for three days at the price of killing him on the fourth.' (Coetzer, 1996, p.121).

Battle of the loop

One dark night, close to the blockhouse lines near Bothaville, a remarkable action was fought. The Cork Militia sent out a patrol along the railway line, but it got lost. A second patrol was ordered to search for it. Looking for the rails of the main line that had been pulled up by the Boers, the first patrol struck a large loop close to the line, which was used for turning trains. They wandered round and around, thinking that they were following the main line. When they considered that they had patrolled enough, they turned around and presently heard a noise in front of them: the second patrol, which had also somehow got onto the loop. Both patrols opened fire at each other. "So the battle was waged round and around the loop, lasting until dawn revealed the entire militia of Cork standing to arms in the Wolvehoek defences a few hundreds yards off. Needless to say this battle, like most others in this war, was entirely bloodless". (Fuller, 1937, pp.160 – 161).

Betrayal

Troopers John Beck and Frederick Nell, amongst other National Scouts, were killed in action by their former comrades of the Heidelberg commando on 24th July 1901 at Braklaagte. They are buried next to each other in the Kloof cemetery, Heidelberg. During the same action Scheepers, Danie Maartens's brother-in-law, was badly wounded. Scheepers and a group of National Scouts had turned his sister and her daughter out of their house in their nightclothes before burning it. They then drove them into the freezing veld in front of their horses for a kilometre before abandoning them. Danie found his wife and child the following morning in a critical condition from the cold. After the Braklaagte action, Danie demanded to see the wounded Scheepers, who was under armed guard. Scheepers crawled towards his sister's husband, begging for mercy. Danie told him that he wouldn't hear any plea, but only wanted to shoot him between the eyes. "He aimed, fired, then climbed on his horse and rode away".

Graves of Troopers Beck and Nell, National Scouts, in the Kloof cemetery, Heidelberg.

Two other turncoats captured during this action, Piet Bouwer and Roelf van Emmenes, were tried and later executed. This was a particularly emotional execution as blood relatives, friends, and ex-pupils of the schoolmaster of Heidelberg, Piet Bouwer, carried it out. (Uys, 1981, p.160 – 165).

Biblical
In Ladysmith it was rumoured that Sir George White was practising the 100th Psalm to mark the 100th day of the Siege. (Griffith, 1974, p.290). I suspect that his eyes were drawn from verse 2: "Worship the Lord with joy; come before him with happy songs!"

to Psalm 102, verses 5 to 7: "I groan aloud; I am nothing but skin and bones. I am like a wild bird in the desert, like an owl in abandoned ruins".

Bitter victory

Of all the Anglo Boer War battlefields that I have visited, I have found Magersfontein to be the most eerie. Sophia Izedinova, who was a volunteer nurse with the Russian-Dutch ambulance serving with the Boers, observed: "In general, in spite of the favourable outcome, this battle had left a dark impression on all the Boers I met who had taken part in it. The resolution of the brave Scotsmen who were shot down by an enemy occupying almost invulnerable positions, greatly astonished the Boers". (Izedinova, 1977, p.139). Captain Trichardt gave a similar report after the Battle. "Our people are calm and quiet and do not exult in the enemy's great loss, but they are determined not to let the enemy pass through them so long as any survive. I cannot describe the battlefield as anything else but an awful slaughter place". (Guest, 1902, p.55).

The remains of a portion of the Boer trench at Magersfontein, south of Kimberley.

Boer qualities

"The Boer has three rare qualities: hospitality, bravery, and a sense of humour. He is the most vigorous, resourceful, and intelligent peasant in the world. There is an old-time courtesy and chivalry about him, owing to his birth, which takes off his hat when he salutes you; yet, at the same time he will not pamper idle women, nor follow the vagaries of a society that less readily forgives an offence against etiquette than an act of dishonour. He is law-abiding and has a reverend regard for custom, and certainly has the best blood in the colonies". (Schikkerling, 1964, p.169).

Bombardment

British artillery support during the Battle of Spion Kop was of more help to the Boers than the British, with the shells falling short and onto the British positions. General Botha reported that some of the Tommies ran across to the Boer positions to escape their own shellfire. (Griffith, 1974, p.262).

As the war progressed the British developed the creeping artillery barrage, whereby their infantry would advance behind the cover

The monument at Bergendal (on the skyline) from Gun Hill, where the British artillery was concentrated.

of bursting shells. The key to the Boer positions at Bergendal was a rocky ridge held by 74 men of the Johannesburg Police. "Against this little ridge, not 90 yards in length and held by about 75 men, nearly 100 cannon were directed, while the English infantry were advancing under fire of their rifles. I thought everything human had perished, even to the lizards and insects in the rent and battered rocks..." (Schikkerling, 1964, p.1). Both sides were astounded that there were still men alive to resist the final infantry charge—in fact 32 survived the bombardment and charge, and escaped over open ground to the rear Boer positions. "On our right stood the farmhouse and from behind it dashed a few mounted Boers; they had to ride through a heavy fire, but as we had been running hard it was rather shaky and did not stop many of them". (Bryant, 1972, p.198).

A British general ordered his guns forward to shell a koppie, which was occupied by Boers. As the guns were being brought into action an officer galloped up to the general to warn him that the Yeomanry had just occupied the hill. 'Occupied the Hill!' exclaimed the General, 'Damn it, man, tell them to get off. How do you expect me to capture it without a bombardment?' (Fuller, 1937 p.245).

General Buller, probably affected by too much sun and champagne, studied the Boer positions from Hussar Hill, which he had ordered Lord Dundonald to capture for observation purposes. He decided that, in order to take Hlangwane, he would first have to take Hussar Hill (on which he was already standing). He accordingly withdrew his force and issued his orders for the next day: "It is intended to seize Hussar Hill tomorrow, and the spurs to the east of it north of Moord Kraal, and to occupy this position with artillery". (Griffith, 1974, p.324). On 14th February 1900, Dundonald duly recaptured the hill. What a pity Buller did not survive to the 1950s, when he could have made an invaluable contribution to *The Goon Show*. Incidentally Winston Churchill's younger brother, John, was shot in the foot during the evacuation of Hussar Hill on 12th February 1900. (Pakenham, 1997, p.347).

Books

Many participants in the war took the Bible with them, which was their constant companion. Fuller describes the library which he took to South Africa: "It consisted of Shakespeare in six minute volumes, the Bible, D'Aguillar's *Maxims of Napoleon*, *Omar Khayyam* and *A Guide to Paris*—which book very soon went through the porthole of my cabin. I read the works of Shakespeare, Tennyson and the Bible from cover to cover, and when at Leeuwpoort Halt, for some reason that I no longer remember, I learned Omar Khayyam by heart". (Fuller, 1937, p.113). Incidentally, my father read Omar Khayyam daily in the Western Desert and Italy during the Second World War, and told me that '... it was an appropriate philosophy at the time.'

By late 1901 General de Wet's mobile library was reduced to *Krieg und Frieden* (a German translation of Tolstoy's *War and Peace*), *Anna Karenina*, a biography of Savonarola, some poetry and theological works, extracts from Seneca, a book on physics, and a history of the American Civil War. (Kestell, 1976, p.214).

C

Camp fire story

The Boers were, and still are, accomplished storytellers. During the trek north through what is now the Kruger National Park to commence the waging of guerrilla warfare, this story was told around the camp fire: "A transport rider was disturbed one night by lions worrying his donkeys, which were tied to the wagon. He decided to hurry away at once and, with his natives, quickly harnessed the animals to the wagon and started forward. As it became light he noticed to his surprise that in the darkness and confusion a lion had been inspanned, and was quietly moving with the team. While thinking furiously they passed some travellers, who shouted to know how he had inspanned the lion. 'Don't ask me,' he replied, 'tell me rather how I can outspan the beast.'" (Schikkerling, 1964, p.85).

Camp site

The remains of the British campsite on the hill above the town of

The British campsite on the hill above Greylingstad with the modern track passing through the tent lines, still visible by the stone circles. The officers' tents are on the left hand side of the main camp and its defensive wall and trench.

Greylingstad can still be clearly seen today. When the veld has been burnt you can make out the tent lines with their protective wall and ditches, the kitchens, the stables, and even the parade ground and the sentries' pathways. Having mapped the whole site, including kilometres of fortifications, I have learned how precisely the camp was laid out. I, therefore, fully appreciate Fuller's comment about the erection of a similar camp at Kroonstad. "Then I had to supervise the pitching of the camp, which was not done with any care for comfort but with a geometric exactness which all but demanded a knowledge of logarithms". (Fuller, 1937 p.134).

Private Tucker was based at Greylingstad from 2nd July 1900 for some months, and continually complained about the fortifications his unit were ordered to erect. After measuring those kilometres of stonewalls in extreme Highveld weather conditions, I share his sentiments. On 17th July 1900, his diary recorded: "Wall building again. We are making this hill like Gibraltar". On 20th July, "Wall building". On 2nd August, "Every day, when not on duty, we are employed wall building or road making from 2.00 pm until 5.00 pm". (Tucker, 1980, pp.122, 125).

Defensive walling above Greylingstad, which Private Tucker helped to build.

A contemporary photograph of British soldiers "Defending the walls".

Civilian bravery

A Boer ambush on the train running from Greylingstad to Heidelberg on 26th August 1900 did not go according to plan. The dynamite exploded after the train had passed, but the Boers opened fire, killing the stoker and wounding the driver [P. Pickering]. In spite of his wounds the driver took the train safely to Heidelberg. (Tucker, 1980, p.129). Mark West, a despatch rider with Thorneycroft's Mounted Infantry, was moved by this incident and wrote the following poem:

> 'Twas on the Transvaal-Natal Railway
> our soldiers lie camping by,
> and their white-bleached tents form a cordon,
> reaching out to the sky.
> 'Twas after the Boer was beaten
> and the winter was dying out,
> yet the nights were dark and stormy
> and foes assailed the rout.
> And often a rail, bridge, or culvert
> would be blasted or torn away.
> And a driver of courage was needed
> to run the first train of the day.

But Driver Phil was ready
to run the first train through.
His hand on the lever was steady
his eye on the line was true.
No thought had he of surrender
when alone and wounded sore.
A gallant and true defender
and a Briton to the core.

He runs through the hills of Greylingstad
he climbs the rise beyond,
and he handles his engine fondly
and well does she respond.
His mate piles on the fuel
as Sugarbosh Rand he nears,
when "halt" rings the startling challenge
and the foe in force appears.
But Driver Phil gripped his lever
and full power on he threw,
he boldly runs the gauntlet
and he runs the first train through.

In the early dawn came the Dutchman
to capture the first train through,
but Driver Phil was on them
ere their fell work they do.
Then in baffled rage they volley
on the dauntless unarmed man,
and he and his mate fall wounded
Phil tending his mate as he ran.
With his teeth he slows up his engine
his senses fast ebbing, and weak,
and when on to the platform he staggers
'my mate' is all he can speak.

But Driver Phil was ready
to run the first train through.

His hand on the lever was steady
his eye on the line was true.
No thought had he of surrender
when alone and wounded sore.
A gallant and true defender
and a Briton to the core.

Mark West added the following note after his poem: "With reference to the facts of this story, see the papers of the day, how P. Pickering, an engine driver, drove the train through from Standerton to Heidelberg, in the face of a strong Boer force that tried to intercept him and rob the train. But pluckily he ran the gauntlet and got through although badly wounded, and shot through both his arms, slowing up his train at Heidelberg with his teeth and then falling fainting on the station platform. His foreman was fatally wounded and died. I saw the place of the hold-up a few days afterwards, while running dispatches".

Communication

The first time that radio was used in military operations was during the Anglo Boer War. Ironically, the six radio sets ordered by the Transvaal Republic were intercepted by the British and used by the Royal Navy in their blockade of Delagoa Bay. The equipment had been ordered to link the forts surrounding Pretoria, because the cost of laying underground telephone cable was prohibitive. The British experimented with the wirelesses in the Northern Cape, eventually establishing wireless contact between the Orange and Modder Rivers, to provide early warning of possible Boer attacks. However, atmospheric conditions made reliable communication impossible, and by March 1900, five sets were installed on the Royal Navy cruisers blockading Delagoa Bay. Thus the cruiser *Thetis* became the first ship to be fitted with wireless under wartime conditions. The maritime experiments were successful and, by the end of 1900, it was decided to equip 42 ships and eight shore stations around Britain with radios. (Baker, 1998, p.37).

The British prisoners of war held in the State Model School, Pretoria, used to receive the war news at the same time as President Kruger, via a Mr Patterson in the Telegraph Department and the Miss Cullingworths, who used to signal it from their house to the signalling officer in the school. (Crum, 1903, p.49).

Dr O'Reilly left carrier pigeons with his patients' families on his rounds of the farms near Heidelberg, so that he could be kept informed of their progress. This practice caused suspicion amongst the British troops occupying Heidelberg, and, suspecting that he was passing information to the Boers, he was arrested and deported to Cape Town. (Uys, 1981, p.80).

Heliographs played an important role in communications throughout the Anglo Boer War. These are instruments, which use two round mirrors to reflect the sun's rays in any required direction, and a Morse code key is used to tilt one of the mirrors in order to send messages. One of the Boer heliographs was captured from the Jameson Raiders in 1896, and this was later

Issuing oil for signalling lamps.

found buried with other equipment at the end of the Anglo Boer War. This heliograph can be seen in the Royal Signals Museum and is marked "Jameson 1896" on its upper edge. The instrument reached its peak efficiency during the Anglo Boer War, with speeds of up to 16 words per minute. Depending on the size of the mirror (there were 3-inch, 5-inch and 10-inch mirror heliographs in service with the British Army), the heliograph had a range of nearly 100 miles. In 1935 a South African record was obtained by a South African artillery unit when, using a 5-inch heliograph, they sent a signal 96 miles, from Massamnekop in Botswana to Pilansberg in the Transvaal. Heliographs were used during the First and Second World Wars, and the last recorded use of the heliograph under active service conditions was in 1941, at the siege of Sollum Hayata in the Western Desert. (Harfield, 1981, pp.4–6).

One of the causes of the British defeat at Spion Kop was the lack of communication between the Kop and General Warren's headquarters. One of the two heliographs on the summit was smashed by a bullet early in the fight, and the other was in too

British Field Telegrapher, in a pose reminiscent of a laid-back Telkom employee.

exposed an area to be used. Flag signals were almost impossible to read owing to the smoke on the summit, and someone had forgotten to run a telephone line between headquarters and the Kop, although the equipment was available. In contrast, General Botha was well briefed on the situation, as his heliographer had set up his equipment below Aloe Knoll as soon as the sun broke through the morning mist. (Ransford, 1969, pp.72, 76, 78). At night, the British could not signal from Spion Kop with their lamps because the oil had either run out, or not been brought at all. (Coetzer, 1996, p.139).

The first ever use of the telephone to direct a battle took place on 6th January 1900, during the Boer attack on Wagon Hill. The main headquarters at Ladysmith was connected with the headquarters of each defence point, and these were in turn connected to the outlying pickets. (Coetzer, 1996, p.59).

Coffee breaks

After destroying the farm of Commandant Fourie, the English officers demanded coffee from his daughter. She brewed it and served it herself, and when asked why she did not use her servant replied: 'Because I know that when our people hear that I served you coffee in the ruins of the property, you will pay with an extra life for every cup I have poured.' (Izedinova, 1977, p.181).

Schikkerling and his commando took pity on the recently released British prisoners of war making their weary way from Nooitgedacht to Waterval Boven, as the Boers were retreating down the railway line. "We made many kettlefuls of coffee for distribution, and handed them out as they passed. The Tommies relished it greatly, some of them even lapping up the grounds". (Schikkerling, 1964, p.60).

Compassion

When General Botha heard that Major Doveton was dying in Ladysmith, he sent an ambulance cart and an escort to fetch Mrs Doveton to see her husband. She arrived before he died, and was with him at the end. (Griffith, 1974, p.292).

Seventy years after the war when Mr Prinsloo, who fought for the Boers, was asked to recall what happened when the British crossed a single pontoon bridge across the Tugela, under heavy Boer fire, he said: 'Now then, I must go slowly, so that I don't cry. So that I don't cry. That was a very sad business, a cruel affair.' (Griffith, 1974, p.311).

Concentration camps

The Boer remedies for illness exacerbated the horror of the concentration camps. "It was to this hospital that in July last the unfortunate children were brought, whose mother had painted them with common green oil paint as a remedy for measles. There were three of these children, one died in the tent; the other two were brought into hospital, but their lives could not be saved.

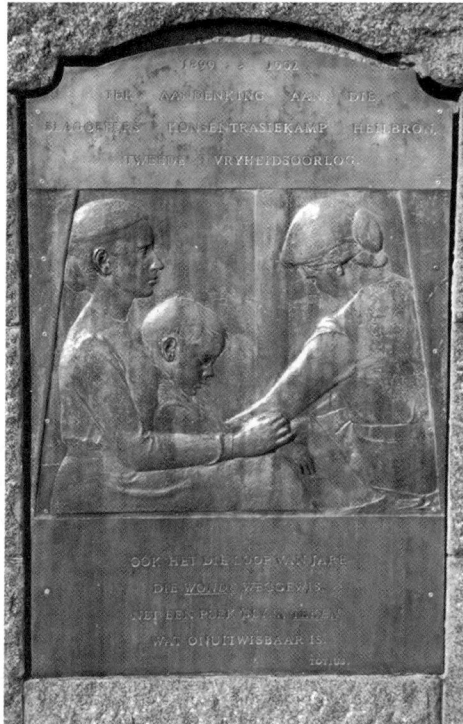

The Heilbron Concentration Camp memorial with a touching quote by the Afrikaans poet, Totius.

They died from the effect of arsenic poisoning. Not content with painting their bodies, the mother had, in the case of one child, added a plaster of American cloth thickly daubed with the same paint. The nurses told us that it was very common among the Boers to tar a patient's feet as a remedy for fever. Dogs' blood was recommended for fits and so on. The nurses spoke of one case where a child in a tent was in a high fever (temperature 104) from measles. The mother utilized the heat thus generated by putting the bread, which she had just made, inside the child's bed to cause it to rise". (C. Paper, 1902, p.126).

Petrus Jacobs (who had surrendered before the guerrilla phase of the war), escaped from the Turffontein Concentration Camp in Johannesburg, and delivered a letter from another camp inmate to his cousin who was serving with the Heidelberg Commando. (Uys, 1981, p.117).

The myth that civilians were imprisoned in the concentration camps still persists today. Evidence from the British Command Papers disproves this. "A good many people have obtained permission to live in town with their relations". (C. Paper, 1902, p.127).

Concentration Camp graves, old Krugersdorp cemetery.

"The camp people also come into Krugersdorp and spend money in the shops there. In one very good tool shop which we visited the man spoke bitterly of the camp women coming in and spending 'money by the sovereign'." (C. Paper, 1902, p.125).

Walter Mears of the Scouting Corps (who succeeded Danie Theron as Commandant) used to visit his fiancée in the Pietermaritzburg Concentration Camp, disguised in British uniform. (Uys, 1981, p.127).

A visit to the concentration camp at Krugersdorp resulted in some interesting observations. "In one very smartly furnished tent with carved oak and red velvet chairs the woman had chickens and guinea pigs inside, the latter of which she was feeding on raw carrots. She was very cheerful and conversational, and said she had plenty of chickens when she first came to camp, but '...though they only had two feet to start with, in camp they quickly got four'." (C. Paper, 1902m, p.127).

Confusion
When Veld-kornet Slabbert fell off his horse, he was dragged along the ground at a gallop for 200 yards, his foot caught in the stirrup. On being asked whether he was still conscious, the first man on the scene replied: 'He don't know his arse from a hole in the ground!' (Schikkerling, 1964, p.259).

Cricket
When Lieutenant Egerton was directing the fire of his 4.7-inch naval guns at Ladysmith, a shell came through the battery's earthworks and hit the young man across both his legs. His comment was: 'This will put a stop to my cricket, I'm afraid.' (Crow, 1903, p.199). This put a stop to more than his cricket as he died later that day, after having both his legs amputated.

On the 101st day of the siege the Boers heliographed a message to Ladysmith: "101 not out". The Manchester Regiment promptly replied: "Ladysmith still batting". (Macdonald, 1999, p.232).

When a Long Tom shell narrowly missed the gun-trail of a 12-pound naval gun at Caesar's Camp, a naval gunnery lieutenant remarked: 'They've put on a new bowler!' (Griffith, 1974, p.291).

Crossfire

The Boers became adept at guerrilla fighting tactics, one of their favourites being a night attack. Almost without exception the proportion of British casualties was much greater than that of the Boers. However, things went wrong during the night attack on Colonel Park at his temporary camp near Dullstroom, on 19th December 1901. The plan was that Commandant Groenewald would fire on the enemy from a good position to the east, whilst Commandant Trichardt would take a position to the west on the top of the mountain. Assistant Commandant-General Muller would set up his pom-pom in the South and fire into the camp. Under no circumstances were the commandos to storm the position, but if the opportunity arose all burghers would storm from the same direction. In his eagerness Commandant Trichardt and his Middelburg Commando stormed the camp and were caught in crossfire from the other two Boer positions, which resulted in

The British military cemetery at Klein Zuikerboskop (also known as Elandspruit and Ouhoutbossie), between Dullstroom and Lydenburg.

eight Boers killed against the British tally of nine. (Muller, 1936, p.154). Today the small cemeteries can still be seen on opposite sides of the road between Dullstroom and Lydenburg, the British on the northern side and the Boer cemetery on the southern side of the road. About 16 years ago flowers appeared in the British cemetery together with a copy of Rudyard Kipling's poem *Recessional.* Standing in the small and lonely British cemetery, one recalls the first two verses of the poem:

> *God of our fathers, known of old,*
> *Lord of our far-flung battle-line,*
> *Beneath whose awful Hand we hold,*
> *Dominion over palm and pine—*
> *Lord God of Hosts, be with us yet,*
> *Lest we forget—lest we forget!*

> *The tumult and the shouting dies;*
> *the Captains and the Kings depart:*
> *Still stands thine ancient sacrifice,*
> *An humble and a contrite heart.*
> *Lord God of Hosts, be with us yet,*
> *Lest we forget—lest we forget!* (Eliot, 1963, pp.139 – 140).

Cruelty to animals

The British destroyed captured enemy livestock by bayoneting them, and some of the soldiers learnt to enjoy this terrible task. After they were ordered to stop killing sheep, a British soldier was caught by his officer standing over a sheep that he had just bayoneted. "Under the officer's eye he looked severely at the prostrate beast, and remarked: 'I will teach you to attempt to bite a British soldier!'" (Schikkerling, 1964, p.192).

D

Deception

Even though the British force based at Dundee had just won the Battle of Talana Hill, they realized that they would have to escape the encircling Boer forces by means of a four-day forced march to Ladysmith. The 4,000 men under General Yule left camp undetected on the night of 26th October 1899, having left lighted candles in their tents. (Griffith, 1974, p.60).

Colonel Baden-Powell built a system of 60 sandbag forts to defend his 11-km perimeter at Mafeking. Hundreds of mines (small black boxes) were placed in the front lines and connected by wires to his observation post. A mine was publicly exploded, with impressive effect, but no one suspected that the boxes were filled with sand. (Bateman, 1977, p.85).

British soldiers manning a sandbag fort.

Colonel Knox sited a battery of guns near the racecourse in Ladysmith, which the Boers repeatedly shelled. The guns never replied as they were made from wood and canvas. (Griffith, 1974, p.117).

The Boer women of Heidelberg were determined that the British troops about to occupy their town would not drink water from the town spring, so they built a Dutch oven over it. During the British occupation they baked bread in the oven daily, and the British never suspected that the oven concealed a spring. The long stone oven can still be seen in the park at the corner of H. F. Verwoerd and Venter Streets.

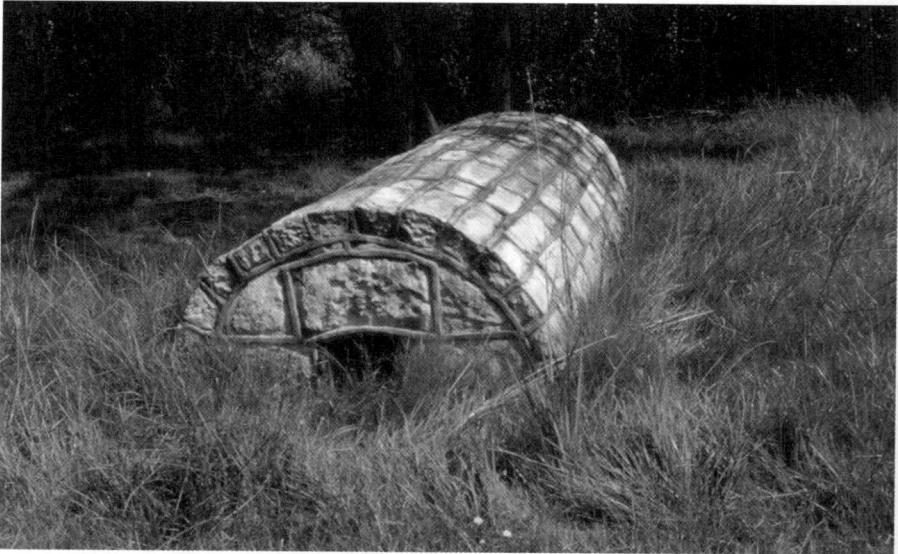

The Dutch oven at Heidelberg, built to hide the spring before the British occupied the town.

During the night attack on Lombards Kop near Ladysmith, which resulted in a Long Tom being disabled, the British were challenged near the summit by a Boer sentry. At the loud 'Fix bayonets!' command the Boers ran away. The soldiers did not in fact have bayonets, and had tapped their rifle butts against rocks to imitate the dreaded sound. (Uys, 1981, p.18).

The British were often misled by white flags and false bugle calls. Before the Battle of Spion Kop, Buller warned his troops to be on their guard for this type of deception. (Coetzer, 1996, p.127).

Commandant Mears and Veld-kornet Kamffer moved into position one night for a dawn attack on a mission station at Beerlaagte. In order to be mistaken for cattle, if detected by the enemy, the men draped wildebeest skins over themselves and lay down next to their horses, holding their reins in one hand. (Uys, 1981, p.197).

Demotion
Commandant Jan Weilbach, who led the Heidelberg Commando into Natal, was removed from command in June 1900 after repeated cowardice. He had failed to support the attack on Dundee on 20th October 1899; ignored an order to assist General Lukas Meyer before the Battle of Nicholson's Nek on 27th October 1899; and was temporarily suspended for failing to protect the Long Tom on Lombards Kop [Ladysmith], which was disabled by the British during their successful night attack on 7th December 1899. At Brandkop, the last defensive position before Bloemfontein, Weilbach abandoned his position before even trying to engage the Greys under Major Allenby. Weilbach was finally dismissed after prematurely abandoning his positions at Irene, during the Battle of Ses Myl Spruit, which led to the surrender of Pretoria. (Uys, 1981, pp.12, 19, 41, 54).

Depression
Cor van Gough, brother of Vincent (the famous painter), committed suicide whilst in a British POW camp. He had served with the Boers, in the "International Legion", which was made up of volunteers from all parts of the world. (Bateman, 1977, p.66).

During the course of his research into the Battle of Bergendal my friend, Huffy Pott, visited the military cemetery near Airlie Station in the Elands Valley. After complaining about the overgrown state of the cemetery to the National Monuments

The overgrown headstone of Maj MacGregor near Airlie station, in the Elands Valley between Waterval Onder and Nelspruit.

Council, Huffy later visited the manager of the farm, Geoff York, at Ryton Estates to find out exactly where the Nooitgedacht prisoner of war camp had been. Unknown to him the National Monuments Council had written to Geoff and asked him to clean up the cemetery. Geoff showed him the letter and then told him a "ghost story". The last grave in the cemetery records that Major R. L. MacGregor, 1st Battalion the Royal Scots, died there on 2nd April 1901. Geoff and his wife Anita walked down to the cemetery to ensure that it had been cleared properly, and took their Jack Russell terrier with them. He smartly examined each grave, sniffed here and there, and lifted his leg a few times. When he got to the last grave, he froze, growled menacingly, and all the hackles on his neck rose. Geoff and Anita thought he had seen a snake, but the area had been cleared and they could see no reason for his aggressive behaviour. Suddenly he turned and, with tail between his legs, ran away. This is when Geoff said, 'He must have seen a ghost!'

A few weeks later they saw an elderly couple poring over a large book opposite the cemetery. Thinking they were lost, they asked if they could help. The elderly couple said that they had just visited the cemetery, and told them that Major MacGregor, in the last grave, had committed suicide. A few months later Huffy's White River friend, James MacGregor, revealed that Major MacGregor was his great uncle, and he still had correspondence about his death at his home, Lochaber. James found a letter from Lieutenant-Colonel William Douglas, the commanding officer of the Royal Scots Regiment, explaining the circumstances leading to the suicide. It revealed that his great uncle was depressed, and being undiagnosed and without help, the Major shot himself. It turned out that there was a history of depression in the family, so we conclude that, through Huffy, the Major was passing this message on.

This story has a strange sequel. Huffy was looking for pictures of horses in Wilson's books entitled *With the Flag to Pretoria* and *After Pretoria—the Guerrilla War*. There are 1724 pages in these four volumes and, putting Lieutenant-Colonel Douglas's letter to one side, he chanced to open volume 3 page 585. Instead of finding a picture of a horse he found a photograph of Lieutenant-Colonel William Douglas, whose letter he had just put aside. Huffy had unwittingly become a cog in the supernatural wheel that linked the Major with his great nephew, and brought the family history of depression to his attention.

Devotion

Every September, since 1901, a package arrived at the Post Office in Chrissiemeer (Lake Chrissie) in the Eastern Transvaal, addressed to "The Postmaster", with no accompanying note, or even return address. The package contained a sprig of heather: one year bound with a blue ribbon, the next with a pink ribbon. Instructions were passed from Postmaster to succeeding Postmaster that the heather was to be placed on the grave of Lieutenant Arthur William Swanston of the Inniskilling Dragoons who died in action near Lake Banagher on 18th October 1900, while trying to save the life of Private J. Garlick. My informant, Tannie Rensie Kruger, the Postmistress from 1947 to 1957, for ten years placed the sprig of heather on Arthur's grave. In 1957,

Left: The headstone of Lt Swanston at Chrissiemeer. Right: "Tannie Rensie" Kruger, the Postmistress of Chrissiemeer, who took over from her predecessors and placed the heather on Lt Swanston's gave between 1947 and 1957.

just before she left Chrissiemeer, she received a note with the package, which she translated from English with much difficulty. The sender revealed that she had been Arthur's fiancée and that she had never married, but was now very sick and thought that this would be the last time she would send heather for her beloved's grave. However, the package continued to arrive for the next two years and Tannie Rensie's successor did her duty.

This touching act of devotion over a period of 60 years is all the more remarkable for the trust placed in the Afrikaans-speaking Postmasters who, understandably, carry bitter memories of the British policies of farm burning and concentration camps carried out during the war. Giving credit to the postal services of the time, Tannie Rensie commented: 'Not a single flower of heather was ever damaged.'

Dirty ending

During a skirmish near Belfast in February 1901, a British soldier took shelter behind a tree from Boer rifle fire. His pet monkey, which had followed him, sat above him in a branch of the tree and, being scared and excited, he regularly relieved himself on the soldier's head. The soldier was permanently put out of his misery when a powerful bullet passed through the tree. (Schikkerling, 1964, p.156). The letter of sympathy sent to his family must have made interesting reading.

Disgrace

The Boers were the first side to suffer the disgrace of losing their guns to the enemy, when two 75-mm guns were overrun at Elandslaagte on 21st October 1899. However, the gunners had served them to the last and even General Kock (who led the invasion of Natal) was fatally wounded defending them. (Mcfadden, 1999, p.27). These guns were later used in the defence of Ladysmith. (Griffith, 1974, p.80).

At the Battle of Colenso on 15th December 1899, the British lost 10 guns of the Royal Field Artillery under the command of Colonel Long. General Buller placed the blame squarely on Long's shoulders as he had deployed his guns too far forward, and commented that he was 'Sold by a damned Gunner.' The Historian, Darryl Hall, analysed the remarkable chain of events leading to the loss of the guns and concluded that it was Long who should have said: 'Sold by a damned General.' Firstly, Buller ordered him to take personal charge of the guns instead of being at his rightful place with General Buller, where he could have exercised overall control of the artillery. Secondly, through inadequate reconnaissance, the British were unaware of the Boers' presence at Fort Wylie; a position that enabled them to enfilade Long's position. Long was ordered to shell the Boer positions in the trenches and hills north of the Tugela, but ended up expending nearly all of his ammunition in trying to neutralize the rifle fire from Fort Wylie. Whilst Long admitted that he had positioned his guns about 300 yards too far forward, the expected infantry support was not forthcoming. When he ran out of ammunition his surviving men were ordered to take cover in a

Concrete plinths marking the position of the guns that were abandoned at Colenso. The reeds on the right hand side of the photograph are in the donga where the survivors of the disaster took shelter.

nearby donga and with the ammunition finally on its way, Buller interfered and ordered it back.

Once he started interfering he couldn't stop and personally directed the attempts to save the guns; he withdrew the supporting naval guns; gave up the whole infantry attack, and withdrew the soldiers who were protecting the guns. No orders were given to disable the guns and it was an easy matter for the Boers to cross the river and capture them. General Botha, who directed the Boer defence, later claimed that Long had in fact saved the British Army that day because, if the infantry attack had gone ahead, the troops would have been decimated in a carefully planned "killing ground". In fact, it was the 7th Battery (well to the right of Long) whose attack on Hlangwane Hill caused the Boers to reveal their positions before the infantry on the British right flank entered the trap. (Hall 1, 1999, 62, 65 – 66, 86, 98, 121 to 123).

British officers in disgrace were sent to the main base at Stellenbosch in the Cape, which gave rise to the expression "to be

Stellenbosched". Colonel Gough was one of the first to be Stellenbosched, as a result of a disastrous reconnaissance mission near Orange River Station. He took it badly, and ended up shooting himself. (Pakenham, 1997, p.179). Here is an excerpt from Kipling's poem entitled *Stellenbosch*:

> *And it all went into the laundry,*
> *But it never came out in the wash.*
> *We were sugared about by the old men*
> *(Panicky, perishing old men)*
> *That hamper and hinder and scold men*
> *For fear of Stellenbosch!* (Eliot, 1963, p.232).

Divine message

In the early morning of 7th February 1901, Maggie Biccard woke up in the Concentration Camp at Howick to hear an angelic choir singing her husband's favourite hymn. She knew that something had happened to Johnny. Two weeks later she heard that her husband had been killed during the night attack on Lake Chrissie. (Uys, 1981, p.111). Co-incidentally, Lake Chrissie was named after Maggie's mother, Christina, daughter of the Voortrekker Andries Pretorius. (Uys, 1981, p.106).

Doubtful hospitality

A Boer named Pienaar unexpectedly came across two British soldiers in the bush. In his excitement, forgetting the words for "hands up" and being a hospitable man, he shouted out, 'Come in, Come in!' (Schikkerling, 1964, p.214).

Drill

General Hart's Irish Brigade fell in for the attack on Colenso at 03h30, and having drilled them for half an hour he marched them in parade-ground style to the Tugela River, leading many of them to their deaths. (Griffith, 1974, p.183).

British troops marching to the relief of Colesburg in a similar formation to General Hart's troops being marched into battle at Colenso.

E

Earthquake

Before the Battle of Bergendal, both sides experienced an earthquake. According to Jack van den Heever of the Heidelberg Commando, "The tremor was brief, but so violent that some of the stones rolled off the schanzes. It was a new phenomenon to most of us. Although I did not hear it, some of the burghers told me that they had heard a rumbling like thunder in the distance". (Uys, 1981, p.69). Deneys Reitz reported that the earthquake occurred during the second day of the British artillery bombardment (26th August 1900). "It came with a loud rumbling and the ground rocked beneath us like a ship, while stones fell from the works, causing much alarm, for disturbances of this kind are practically unknown in South Africa. We thus suffered a bombardment from above and an earthquake from below at one in the same time, and this remained a topic for wondering discussion months afterwards". (Reitz, 1929, p.120).

Escape

Both Winston Churchill and Captain Aylward Haldane (who was the officer in charge of the train) were captured after the Boers ambushed the armoured train at Chieveley. They both later escaped from the Staats Model School in Pretoria, where they were held prisoner. The details of Churchill's escape are well known, but Haldane had a more interesting (or should I say boring) time. After Churchill's escape the officers were advised that they would shortly be moved to a more secure prison. Captain Haldane and a non-commissioned officer hid under a tiny trap door in the wooden floor. Unable to stand, and having over-estimated the Boers' efficiency, they remained there for weeks, being fed by three officers who shared their secret. Eventually the prisoners were moved and, with the building deserted, the two made their escape by rail to Delagoa Bay. (Lowry, 1902, p.143).

The Staats Model School in Pretoria.

When a Boer called John Logan sneaked through the British lines into Lydenburg in an attempt to free General Viljoen, he stumbled against a sentry in the dark, and in order to be taken for an English officer, he swore most terribly at the soldier for not saluting. The Tommy apologized and Logan escaped. (Schikkerling, 1964, p.368).

Cornelius Spruyt was captured on 19th February 1900, during the early phase of the Battle of Paardeberg. On his way to Cape Town he managed to untie himself and jumped out of the speeding train. Hiding during the day and marching at night, he arrived at Colesburg four days later. (Uys, 1981, p.38). Another member of the Heidelberg Commando captured at Paardeberg, Charlie Brink, escaped in Cape Town and boarded a Russian ship, which took him to Lourenco Marques. (Uys, 1981, pp.38, 50).

At Moordenaar's Poort in the Northern Cape, General Smuts took three commandos with him on a recce of the nearby British positions. He returned later on his own, on foot, having escaped an ambush that saw his three companions killed. (Reitz, 1929, pp.210 – 211). With hindsight, the British were lucky that he escaped, as in later life he became Prime Minister of South Africa and a staunch supporter of the Empire in both World Wars.

During his invasion of the Cape, Smuts's Commando was completely surrounded on a plateau, with all the exits guarded. That night, whilst they were preparing for a "last stand" in the morning, a local hunchbacked cripple volunteered to guide the commando out of the trap. He led them along a boggy path, within earshot of the British sentries, and led them to the steep escarpment. As Reitz reports, "We now began to descend what was probably the nearest approach to the vertical attempted by any mounted force during the war... At times whole batches of men and horses came glissading past, knocking against all in their course..." (Reitz, 1929, pp.218 – 219).

Just after this incident the British cavalry commander, General French, had a lucky escape. The train, on which he was travelling to control operations on the plateau, passed Smuts's Commando in the dead of night. Smuts forbade his men to fire on the train in case civilians were injured, and French raced past in the dark, unaware of the danger. (Reitz, 1929, p.220).

At his camp at Nooitgedacht, between Rustenburg and Pretoria, General Clements sited his six-ton 4.7-inch naval gun on the hillside facing the valley, and neglected to give orders to the artillerymen to clear a field of fire in the bush. In the event Generals Smuts and Beyers attacked the camp from the top of the hill, and the gun was pointing the wrong way. Whilst the Boers were looting the camp, the gun's commander, Major Inglefield, tried to rescue the gun with nine of the 16 surviving oxen from his gun team. The oxen refused to climb the hill and Inglefield had to think of something else. "Out of the disaster emerged a kind of comic miracle: Inglefield's gun-crew heaved the great gun bodily round in its emplacement; it shook itself free, rose like a great elephant from the mimosa scrub, rolled down the hill, gathering speed, every Mauser levelled at it; now it was travelling fast; it thundered through the camp; and at length Inglefield, the triumphant mahout, roped it up and conducted it safely onwards to Yeomanry Hill". (Pakenham, 1997, p.479).

A view of the hillside where the 4.7-inch Naval gun was sited, from the summit of Nooitgedacht. Yeomanry Hill, to which the surviving British troops retreated, can be seen on the left-hand side of the photograph in the middle distance.

General Broadwood's column launched a pre-dawn attack on the town of Reitz on 11th July 1902, and succeeded in capturing most of the Free State government. President Steyn was warned just in time by his servant, Ruiter. He fled to the stables, without his jacket and with his nightcap on his head, and hurriedly saddled his horse. "Without bridle or bit, and with only the riem of the halter in the horse's mouth, the President galloped away. A soldier followed and shot at him; but the President's horse was fresh, and gained on the tired steed of the soldier, until he was out of danger". (Kestell, 1976, p.194).

Executions
On 20th March 1900, General Piet Joubert was sentenced to death at a Council of War at Kroonstad, according to P.J. Pretorius. The

Commandant General of the Transvaal Republic was accused of deliberately letting opportunity slip by allowing General Yule to escape from Dundee unmolested; failing to follow up his victory at Nicholson's Nek when he had the opportunity of decimating an army of 10,000 men in full flight; and disregarding sound advice to push on to Durban when he had the chance. This may have forced Britain to sue for peace. After the relief of Ladysmith, Joubert was censured along with eight other generals present at the Council of War at Glencoe Station because only two generals were present during the retreat: Botha and Meyer. (Viljoen, 1903, p.121).

Among the generals present at the Kroonstad Council of War, according to Pretorius and De Wet (De Wet, 1902, p.79), were Botha, Delarey, De Wet and of course Joubert. However, Professor Barnard denies that he was present. It was General Botha who placed a Mauser bullet and a glass of poison in front of Joubert and told him, 'Take your choice!' These words were also heard by two guards outside the tent, Ellis and Swart. Joubert said, 'I do not see the opportunity of a bullet', and then requested that his family be kept in the dark as to his sentence. He then stood up, drank the poison, and walked back to his chair. As he reached it, he dropped in his tracks and died. (Pretorius, 1996, pp.65 – 66).

Is this a true account of Joubert's death or just speculation? My fellow historians are doubtful. According to Todd and Fordham, "Piet Joubert, the old and cautious Commandant-General, was taken ill immediately after the Council of War and forced to retire to his farm. There, on 27ᵗʰ March 1900, he died". (Tucker, 1980, p.96). Trew adds that Joubert left the Council of War with a severe cold. Presidents Kruger and Steyn were present at the Council of War, at least on 17ᵗʰ March 1900. (Jones, 1999, p.128; Trew, 1999, p.152). Why does Pretorius not mention the presence of both the Presidents at the meeting, unless they left the problem to their generals to sort out (by court-martial) after their premature departure? Also, why did the generals present never, in later years, disclose what really happened at the Council of War? In 1893 Kruger narrowly defeated Joubert in the presidential elections, but Joubert (the hero of Majuba) was still held in high esteem by the Boers. Was the Council of War a means to eliminating a serious rival? What was Kruger's real message at Joubert's State Funeral when he said, ' He died as he has lived, on the path of *duty* and honour...'? (Tucker, 1980, p.96—my italics).

   In my opinion, contemporary accounts point to the fact that there was some skulduggery at the Council of War. Various sources quote the date as the 17th March, others say the 20th March. One of the questions that was settled at the Council of War was that it was Joubert's wish that Louis Botha should succeed him as Commandant-General. (Trew, 1999, p.152). General Viljoen later wrote: "And if I am not mistaken, this was the first announcement of the important fact that Botha was to lead us in future". (Viljoen, 1903, p.122). The political matter of succession settled (and why did politicians and not the commandant-generals preside at the meeting, as is customary?), it seems as though the Presidents left the meeting and Joubert was tried, sentenced and executed, and his body was probably smuggled to Pretoria. It is also interesting to note that Viljoen had put forward a motion at Kroonstad, "That all the generals be asked to resign, with the exception of one assistant-general and one fighting-general". (Viljoen, 1903, p.121). We will probably never know what really happened at Kroonstad. Viljoen commented that, 'Much more was said and much arranged.' (Viljoen, 1903, p.123). General de Wet said, 'I shall not enter upon all that happened at that meeting.' (De Wet, 1902, p.79). A cover-up?

When the commandos in the Eastern Transvaal received the news of the execution of Commandant Scheepers in the Cape Colony, Schikkerling commented: 'This is the sort of thing that makes enemies bad friends.' (Schikkerling, 1964, p.362).

In August 1901 the Bush Veldt Carbineers shot 12 Boer prisoners of war on the orders of their officers. One English and five Australian officers were court-martialled and two of the Australian officers, Lieutenants Handcock and Morant, were found guilty and executed. Because this was an Australian unit there was a great political outcry in that country. However, Kitchener had to take extreme action against this kind of indiscipline in his army. (Pakenham, 1997, p.539). Lieutenants Handcock and Morant are buried in Pretoria's old cemetery in Church Street within consecrated ground. This is unusual, as the practice at the time was to bury executed soldiers in unconsecrated ground.

Commandant Groenewald was trying to dislodge some armed Blacks from a cave in the Steenkampsberg, when he was shot in the back. His men were so enraged that they caught one of the Blacks and stoned him to death. (Schikkerling, 1964, p.367).

After the war a member of the occupying British garrison in Pretoria, Private Letchford, was court-marshalled and executed for misappropriating canteen funds. He was buried in the cemetery at Roberts Heights on 20th November 1912, in unconsecrated ground. In subsequent years his headstone had to be repaired repeatedly, because lightning kept striking it. His family took up the case and, with proper legal representation, he

Left: The memorial to Lieutenants Handcock and Morant in the old Church St. cemetery, Pretoria. Right: Private Letchford's headstone in the military cemetery at Roberts Heights, Pretoria.

was found to be innocent and his name was cleared. Letchford's grave was then consecrated and the fence was extended to incorporate his grave into the cemetery. After this, the lightning strikes stopped.

Exposure under fire

During the fourth attempt to relieve Ladysmith a Royal Artillery officer, Major Caldwell, was calmly directing fire from his deck chair, with Boer shells falling all around him. When asked why he did not take cover he replied, 'It's not our way.' (Griffith, 1974, p.328).

Contrast this with the Boer artilleryman's fear of reprisals from the British gunners. Macdonald watched their gunners prepare and load the gun, and then retire on horseback a quarter of a mile to the rear. The gunner appointed to fire the gun had a long lanyard and a fast horse. He withdrew about 200 yards, pulled the lanyard, and then galloped back to his companions. (Macdonald, 1999, p.23).

F

Fair warning

An early warning about a planned Boer attack on Ladysmith was taken seriously, when every fighting man was put under arms. The warning came in a curiously roundabout way. A Frenchman serving with the Boers got word of the planned attack and, believing that this would lead to the fall of Ladysmith and a devaluation of the pound, decided to invest on the Paris Stock Exchange. An English stockbroker in Paris bought the information and sent it to his partner in London, who informed the War Office, who cabled Buller, who passed on the warning to Sir George White. (Griffith, 1974, p. 288).

Whenever they could the Boers prepared themselves for an attack on the enemy by saying prayers and singing hymns. At midnight on 5th January 1900, the Imperial Light Horse picket on the southern side of Wagon Hill heard the Boers singing hymns, but attached no significance to this. Three hours later the Boer attack on Wagon Point took place. (Griffith, 1974, p. 13).

A view of Wagon Point from Wagon Hill, Ladysmith.

Father and son
After the Battle of Elandslaagte, a stretcher-bearer came across a dying old white-haired Boer who asked him to try to find his 13 year-old son, who had been fighting beside him. He found the son's body close by and brought him to his father. Hugging his son and moaning to himself, the old Boer died. (Griffith, 1974, p. 6).

A 70 year-old Boer and his grandson fought side by side at Spion Kop. Every time the old Boer hit a British soldier his grandson would remark, 'One more Rooinek down, Oupa!' The next day they were both found dead. (Griffith, 1974, p. 263).

On the skyline, the main British trench at Spion Kop from the Boer position on Aloe Knoll. It was from here that Boer marksmanship won them the day.

As the sun set on 28th November 1899, General Delarey's 19 year-old son, Adriaan, was hit in the side and the stomach at the Battle of Modder River. Although he himself was wounded, his father carried him into the Boer hospital at Jacobsdal, where Adriaan died an hour later. Two weeks later General Roberts's son, Freddie, was killed at Colenso in an attempt to save Long's guns. These tragedies drew the men together in later years. (Bateman, 1977, p. 78).

Lord Roberts and his son were both awarded the Victoria Cross, the father in India and the son in South Africa.

Prior to the Battle of Bergendal a young artillery lieutenant, F. Rainsford-Hannay, engaged the Boer artillery with two guns of the 21st Battery. Four of his men were wounded by rifle fire and they were running short of ammunition. By coincidence his father, a colonel, had been given permission to visit his son, and arrived at a crucial time. Without any hesitation he assumed the duties of a lowly "No 6", took off his jacket and carried ammunition to the guns under heavy fire. Such an event is without parallel in the history of the Royal Field Artillery.

Fire

Before the Battle of Bergendal, Generals Botha and Viljoen had their headquarters near Dalmanutha Station, which was swept by a veld fire. "When we came to the spot that night we found everything burned save the iron tyres of the wagon wheels, so that the clothes we had on were all we had left us. All my notes had perished, as well as other documents of value. I was thus deprived of the few indispensable things that had remained to me, for at Elandslaagte my kit had also fallen into the hands of the British". (Viljoen, 1903, pp.178 – 179).

The site of the Boer officers' campsite near Dalmanutha station, which was destroyed by a veld fire shortly before the battle of Bergendal.

In 1964 my great-uncle, gunner Archie Wilson, recalled the Battle of Doornkop in a letter to my father. "The big fight for Johannesburg was at Doornkop where my battery took a prominent part. The veld went on fire, and it was difficult to get some of the wounded removed, but of course these things do happen in war". Corporal J.F. McKay of the Gordon Highlanders was awarded the Victoria Cross for repeatedly attending to the wounded at Doornkop, under a withering fire at short range. (Jones, 1999, p. 60).

First command

Lieutenant Fuller's first independent command was at a place called Jordaan Siding, officially known as No. 2 Cossack Post. "The garrison consisted of one officer and 20 men of the 5th Royal Fusiliers—the officer a mere boy and his men little more than children; 18th Mounted Infantry, who presumably were the Cossacks; two signallers, two telephone operators and 27 Black night watchmen, armed with Martini-Henry rifles, who by the soldiery were dubbed the 'Black Watch'. I walked round my command, almost wept over its inefficiency, bought some eggs at the farm, read a chapter or two of *Les Cent Nouvelles*, which cheered me immensely, and then retired to bed to listen to a battle on the railway line between the Black Watchmen, who were blazing away at each other". (Fuller, 1937, pp.113 – 114).

First words

Major Gough was the first British officer to enter Ladysmith after the relief. He knew Sir George White, who greeted him with the words: 'Hello, Hubert, how are you?' (Griffith, 1974, p.358). Gough's Mounted Infantry were humiliated by General Botha 18 months later at Blood River Poort, losing 23 officers and men killed, 21 wounded and 241 taken prisoner (including Gough). (Pakenham, 1997, p.531).

Flight

During the terrifying charge of the 5th Royal Irish Lancers through the Boers fleeing the Battle of Elandslaagte, a Boer threw down his rifle, held his wife's hand and shouted: 'We surrender!' A

Lancer shouted, 'Stick those pigs!' and ran the burgher through, and then his wife. An officer later ordered the Lancers to bury her, and the man who killed her stole her ring. (Griffith, 1974, p. 2).

The Boers retreated from their positions at this vantage point at Elandslaagte, to the Lancers' charge on the plain below.

Football

A Boer shell interrupted a card game and a football match between the Gordon Highlanders and the Imperial Light Horse during the Siege of Ladysmith. Bella Crow (a nurse) wrote in her diary on 18th November 1899, that a Long Tom shell landed in an unoccupied tent, and then buried itself between that tent and the next one, in which a number of men were playing nap. "It scattered dust all over but they never moved, went on playing, so did the footballers". (Bella Crow). A war correspondent observed that, "Under cover of the smoke the Gordons sneaked a goal, and the point as to whether such a contingency is covered by the rules of the game was remitted to English sporting authorities". (Macdonald, 1999, p. 68).

Forgotten

When General Yule abandoned Dundee he forgot to take his

secret papers with him. Their publication caused Britain acute embarrassment, as they contained plans for the invasion of the Transvaal and the Orange Free State, drawn up in 1896 after the Jameson Raid. (Griffith, 1974, p. 66).

Forts

In the field it is fairly easy to distinguish a Boer from a British fort. "... we commenced building a stone fort on an eminence which commands a very wide view. We loosen stones all about and build without mortar or regard to symmetry". (Schikkerling, 1964, p. 337).

Friends

Two close friends had farms in the neighbourhood of Spion Kop: Mr Pretorius and Mr Spearman. At the outbreak of war Pretorius joined the Boer forces, and Spearman the British forces. After Spearman had left, Pretorius collected all of Spearman's valuables and sold them. At the end of the war they both returned to their farms and greeted each other like long-lost brothers. Pretorius then took Spearman to the veld and unearthed the proceeds of the sale, explaining, 'I didn't want either the Boers or the British to rob you.' (Griffith, 1974, p. 244).

Fuel

When Fuller was based at Jordaan Siding he worked out a method of stealing coal from government trains. In order to prevent the theft of coal, an ignorant transport officer had introduced a system of whitewashing each truckload of coal to disguise it. This was a dead giveaway to Fuller's raiding party who waited at a bend in the railway line and, when the train with its load of whitewashed coal was spotted from the bluff, hid in a culvert. As the train passed, two men on one side threw a rope over the train to two men on the other side, and by this means skimmed two or three hundredweight of coal off the truck. (Fuller, 1937, pp. 116 – 117). Fuller remarked that throughout the war it was not so much polluted water as a lack of fuel that was the cause of enteric (typhoid). (Fuller, 1937 p. 144).

Funerals

General Penn-Symons, mortally wounded at Talana Hill, died on 23rd October 1899 in Dundee, a prisoner of the Boers. Many Boers attended the burial service, acting with great reverence, and the Commandant-General sent a letter of sympathy to General White in Ladysmith. (Griffith, 1974, p.65).

While burying the dead after the Battle of Vaalkrans, the funeral party came under shellfire from the Boers. The Minister instructed the men to lie down and calmly and slowly proceeded with the funeral service. One of the soldiers commented afterwards: "That knocked the bottom out of any kind of service I had ever been to before, and I don't know as I'm particular anxious to go to another like it either". (Griffith, 1974, p.318).

Futile loyalty

At the height of the Battle of Spion Kop, when the combatants were shooting at one another at a range of only 20 yards, a Boer's Black servant wandered amongst the rocks looking for the body of his master. In spite of repeated warnings, the servant continued to examine the dead, and was soon shot through the brain. (Reitz, 1929, p.77).

G

Ghosts

On 28th August 1983, whilst conducting field research at the Helvetia battlefield, I stayed at the nearby Ye Wayside Inn in Waterval Onder. In conversation with the owner, Mr Dustin, I asked whether he had heard the story of the ghost of a British officer who meets a nurse under one of the giant bluegum trees near the hotel. Although he had heard the story, he had not heard of any recent sightings. He remarked that was strange that I had raised the subject, as one of the pub regulars had seen a ghost a couple of weeks before my visit. The man had rushed into the pub just after nightfall in a great state of agitation. He had been driving his truck on an old track in the hills at sunset and had stopped to open a farm gate. After exchanging greetings with a well-spoken Englishman who was standing near the gate, he noticed that the man was dressed in an old-fashioned officer's uniform and had a bandage around his head. The officer then disappeared and the farmer drove as fast as he could to the nearest pub, at Ye Wayside Inn.

The British military cemetery at Helvetia battlefield. It was near here that the ghost of Major Cotton was seen.

I established from Mr Dustin that the incident had taken place on the Helvetia battlefield, and I was able to identify the officer as Major Cotton of the King's Liverpool Regiment, who had surrendered two of the Helvetia forts at an early stage during the

Boers' pre-dawn attack. "The officer in command of Middle and South Hills, deprived of judgement by a severe wound in the head, thought nothing worth saving when the gun was lost, and ordered a surrender". (Maurice, 1906 – 1910, vol 4, p.26). Although Major Cotton survived the war it would appear that his ghost visits the scene of his humiliation. The British lost eleven men killed, one officer and 28 men wounded, and four officers and 231 men taken prisoner.

Gifts

The British besieged in Ladysmith thought that the Boers would at least respect Christmas Day; however, a few shells were fired into the town. These failed to explode and, on investigation, were found to be filled with plum-pudding. (Macdonald, 1999, p.141). One of these shells, a Long Tom, is on display at the Ladysmith Museum inscribed "Compliments of the Season".

One of the shells fired into besieged Ladysmith on Christmas Day, 1899, which contained plum pudding. On display at the Ladysmith Museum, this Long Tom shell is inscribed "Compliments of the Season".

Government in exile

The Transvaal Government had to remain mobile during the guerrilla phase of the war. The Treasurer-General was able to load the entire Treasury of paper money ("blue backs") on a mule at any sign of danger. And so the wealth of the State that owned the richest mines in the world could now be accommodated on the back of a single mule—and there was space to spare for a few sundry tin cans. (Schikkerling, 1964, p.232). Contrast this with the wealth of a member of the Fordsburg Commando who accumulated gold at the Glynn Mine, Sabie, by scraping the amalgam off the plates. At this time his wealth amounted to 7 oz of fine gold, 14 pumpkins, biltong, a bottle of lard, and some dried peaches. "Now, like one of Napoleon's defaulting marshals, he dare not tempt fortune by going into battle". (Schikkerling, 1964, p.380).

Graves of unknown soldiers

Surgeon Blake-Knox gives an insight into why some British dead could not be identified. "The identification of soldiers killed in action is very laborious, and quite often impossible. The present identification-ticket is sown in a special pocket in the soldier's tunic; men often take off their coats in action, and they are temporarily mislaid, or their coats may be taken off to dress their wounds". (Coetzer, 1996, p.204 – 205).

Boer commandos were raised by district with family, friends and neighbours serving in the same commando; therefore, there was no need for a formal system of identification. If a Boer found himself fighting with a strange commando, he would have a discussion with his neighbours to find out whether they had mutual acquaintances or relatives to ensure that someone would remember him if he was killed. (Pretorius, 1996, p.143).

Next to the grave of an unknown soldier at Chrissiemeer, is the grave of a Private J. Dow. Even more remarkable: Private Dow's grave is next to that of Lieutenant John Dow, whose memorial was erected by his mother, Grace Dow.

Grave of an unknown soldier and Private J. Dow, Chrissiemeer cemetery.

Gross negligence

The orders for the attack on Spion Kop instructed that only 20 picks and 20 shovels were to be carried to the top in regulation stretchers. Also, that pack mules would carry water in waterproof sheets—which are absolutely useless as water bags. (Coetzer, 1996, p.135).

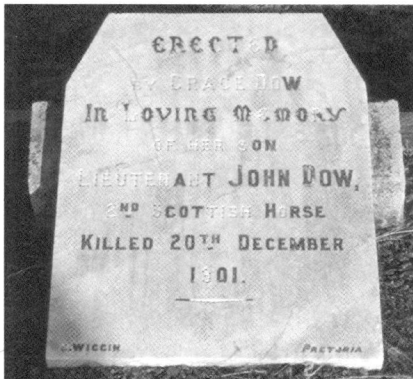

Headstone of Lt John Dow, erected by his mother Grace Dow, Chrissiemeer cemetery.

H

Hand grenades

Schikkerling's Commando made hand grenades by filling the hollow ornamental cast-iron tops of electric posts with dynamite, as well as ink pots and baking powder tins, which were also filled with metal nuts and scraps of iron. (Schikkerling, 1964, p.359).

The Irish members of General Smuts's Commando, with their love of explosives, made hand grenades from dynamite pillaged from the copper mines in the Northern Cape. They were used to good effect in capturing the forts defending the town of Springbok. (Reitz, 1929, p.301 – 304).

Hard of hearing

The British once shelled Doorie Hattingh's farmhouse near the Vaal River. Shells suddenly exploded all around the house, collapsing a wall. With that Doorie's deaf mother-in-law stood up and shouted, 'Doorie, go open the door! Someone's knocking!' (Uys, 1981, p.78).

Hats

After a fierce skirmish General Delarey took off his cap and placed it on the face of a mortally wounded British officer to shield him from the sun. The dying officer requested his friend, Major Tudor-Trevor, to get Delarey the 'best hat that money could buy.' At the end of the war the major carried out his last request and gave Delarey a magnificent top hat. (Orford, 1971, p.1, 64).

During the last part of the war, Boers stripped dead British soldiers of their uniforms because they were desperately short of clothes. A British mounted-infantryman, hotly chased, dropped his Baden Powell-style hat, which his pursuer then stopped to pick up, and by this means saved his entire uniform, if not his life. (Schikkerling, 1964, p.205).

The seer Van Rensburg prophesied his friend General Delarey's death. He saw the number 15 on a dark cloud from which blood issued, and then General Delarey returning home without his hat. Immediately afterwards he saw a carriage approaching covered with flowers. Delarey died on 15th September 1914, having just lost his hat. Incidentally, the date 1914 adds up to15. (Orford, 1971, p.1, 62).

Headless
The flight of the British into Ladysmith after the disaster at Nicholson's Nek was given fresh impetus when a horse of the 5th Lancers galloped past them. "The rider was firmly fixed in the deep cavalry saddle; the reins tossed loose with the horse's mane, and both hands were clenched against either side of his breast. His head was cut off clean at the shoulders". (Griffith, 1974, p.82).

Hiding
After the disaster at Colenso the Boers sent a cheeky message across the Tugela: "How's Mr Buller? When is he coming for his next hiding?" (Griffith, 1974, p.209).

The drift at the Koorn Spruit where General Broadwood's convoy was hijacked on 31st March 1900. The railway station at Sannah's Post is hidden in the trees in the distance.

Hijack

On 31st March 1900, General de Wet ambushed General Broadwood's convoy on the banks of the Koorn Spruit near Sannah's Post, 30 kilometres east of Bloemfontein. The general's brother, Piet de Wet, with about 300 men, hid in the drift on the main road to Bloemfontein. Broadwood had decided to withdraw his wagons and artillery to Bushman's Kop, and the column advanced without taking the precaution of sending out scouts. De Wet allowed the first few wagons to cross unhindered, and then quietly substituted his own drivers for those of the British.

Seeing the orderly progress of the column beyond the drift, the enemy was unaware that it had been hijacked. De Wet himself supervised the crossing of the drift, until matters became confused owing to congestion, and he was obliged to fire the first shot, the signal for the commencement of the fight. In the end De Wet captured 83 supply wagons, seven guns, and 428 prisoners, leaving 159 British dead and wounded on the field. (Schikkerling, 1964, pp.56 – 57; Creswicke, vol. 5, 1902, pp.1 – 15).

Holding hands

When setting explosives under the railway line, to avoid leaving give-away footprints, the Boer sabotage party would walk some distance along the railway lines, one Boer on each line, holding hands for support. (Schikkerling, 1964, p.157).

Hoodwinked

In preparation for the advance on Spion Kop the cunning sailors at Gun Hill near Chieveley, under great secrecy, constructed two dummy 4.7-inch naval guns. When they left Gun Hill on 10th January 1900, they unveiled the dummy guns and took the two real guns with them. They then received a heliograph message from the Boers above Colenso: "Do you take us to be such fools as not to know a dummy from a real gun?" (Griffith, 1974, p.242).

Horseracing

Riding on a borrowed horse with his colonel, Lieutenant Fuller touched "Fat Belly's" flanks and it took off like the wind, with the colonel and his horse in tow. 'Stop that brute, you damned young fool, damn you! Can't you hold her?' shouted the colonel. They passed the escort, they passed through the reserve, they shot through the supports, and flew through the patrols of the advanced guard, arriving at Boschkoppies ahead of the whole column. Expecting a tirade from the colonel when he caught his breath, Fuller was surprised that he started screaming at Captain Williams, who eventually caught up with them. 'You damned idiots! Don't you know the difference between a rearguard and an advanced guard? Why the hell don't you carry out your orders? I have a good mind to put your under arrest!' He then turned to Fuller and exclaimed; 'As for those cavalrymen, they aren't worth a damn!' (Fuller, 1937, pp.137 to 138).

When General Ian Hamilton took Heidelberg on 23rd June 1900, he fell off his horse chasing the defenders and broke his collarbone. (Jones, 1999, p.96).

Horses
Much to their distress the British besieged in Ladysmith were forced by starvation to eat their horses. The Boers heliographed Ladysmith, "How do you like horse meat?" The British replied: "Fine, when the horses are finished we're going to eat Boer". (Macdonald, 1999, p.233).

The Boers entrusted their lives to their horses. "In peaceful times there never can exist that same strong friendship between man and horse as in time of war, more especially in such a purely equine war as ours". (Schikkerling, 1964, p.73). On occasion a horse or mule had to be put out of its misery. "And when the beast in the last stages of exhaustion, could no longer follow and after every device had been tried, rather than leave it to perish of thirst, or be killed by wild beasts, he would shoot it, and then sit weeping". (Schikkerling, 1964, p.73). And from the beast's point of view: "He put four bullets through the beast's head, two from either side, and, as he was coming away, the beast, still living, looked wistfully up at us". (Schikkerling, 1964, pp.49 – 51).

The War Office calculated that over 400,346 horses, mules and donkeys lost their lives during the war. (Pakenham, 1997, p.572). These losses on the British side excluded animals captured from the Boers and those that died in the service of the Boers. (Hall 2, 1999, p.237). It is, therefore, likely that the final casualty figure was in excess of 500,000. "Roberts's grand army swallowed horses as a modern army swallows petrol". (Pakenham, 1997, p.381).

Horsefeed had to be imported from India and South America in great quantities. The legacy from this is both a curse and a delight in South Africa today. "Khaki weed" (Tagetes minuta) is a noxious weed, and cosmos (Bidens formosa), a beautiful autumn flower, both having arrived in the country in the imported hay. (Grabandt, 1985, pp.51, 69).

Tons of imported animal feed stored at the important railway junction at De Aar, Northern Cape.

I

Ian Hamilton's revenge

Ian Hamilton was a lieutenant at the Battle of Majuba during the First Anglo Boer War on 27th February 1881. At the time it was the most humiliating defeat ever inflicted on Britain. Of the approximately 365 British soldiers engaged, there were 280 casualties, including General Colley. The Boers, similar in number, but attacking a seemingly unassailable position, lost one man killed and five wounded. This disaster influenced Hamilton's conduct during the second Anglo Boer War, not only because it left him with a permanently crippled arm, and that his men (the Gordons) had been defeated, but that he believed that the desperate situation could have been saved by a bayonet charge at a crucial point. As the Boers were storming the ridge he tried to organize a counter-attack and ordered his men to fix bayonets.

Majuba Hill, as seen from the Boer laager during the first Anglo Boer War, 1881.

This order was countermanded by his commanding officer, Colonel Hay, and Hamilton took the unusual step of running down to General Colley and appealing to him directly. He saluted and said, 'I do hope, General, that you will let us have a charge, and that you will not think it presumption on my part to have come up and asked you.' Sir George replied: 'No presumption, Mr Hamilton, but we will wait until the Boers advance on us, and then give them a volley and charge.' (Ransford, 1967, pp.101 – 102). Shortly after this the Boers over-ran the British line, and General Colley was killed.

Colonel Ian Hamilton, directing the battle of Wagon Hill during the Siege of Ladysmith, on 6th January 1900, ordered a series of bayonet charges to be made against the Boers who had gained a small foothold there. Captain Codrington of the Imperial Light Horse was the first to charge and die. Major Mackworth was the next to fall in the King's Royal Rifles' charge. Lieutenant Raikes died leading the next charge, followed by Lieutenant Todd who covered three yards before he was killed and seven of his 12 men

Left: Memorial to the men of the Devonshire Regiment who fell during the battle for Wagon Hill, Ladysmith. Right: The Gordon Highlanders' memorial near the Doornkop battlefield.

hit. Finally Major Bowen of the King's Royal Rifles and some of his men were killed in the next charge. (Griffith, 1964, pp.216 – 217).

Colonel Hamilton's obsession with bayonet charges next came to the fore at the Battle of Doornkop on 29th May 1900. In order to take Johannesburg, Hamilton and French with 20,000 men were ordered to outflank the Boer positions to the west. The Boers were entrenched on the ridge in and around the farmhouse where Jameson and his Raiders had surrendered in 1896: an indirect humiliation for Britain, and a direct cause of the Second Anglo Boer War. Here was the chance for revenge for Hamilton and the Gordons. He ordered the City Imperial Volunteers and the Gordon Highlanders to charge the position across open ground without supporting fire or adequate cover from the artillery. The CIV took proper cover and suffered few casualties; however, the Gordons reverted to tradition. "'Advance!' The front line got up, and walked slowly forwards down the slope. 'Advance!' and another kilted line rose and followed them; and then another. The lines were widely separated and there were gaps of about 15 yards between each man and the next; otherwise, the advance was conducted with the same drill-book tactics as Hamilton had used at Elandslaagte (and, indeed, Raglan at Balaclava). ...Then, there was a gasp and murmur among the watchers. Against the backdrop of burnt veld, sparkling in the sun, the ripple of steel. Fix bayonets! The figures gained the skyline, a few at first, then more. There was a sharp, rapid exchange of shots, then the firing flickered and died away. The Gordons had the hill. They had lost 100 men in ten minutes, but they had done the trick". (Pakenham, 1997, p.425). The loss of life from this unnecessary frontal attack was much criticized because General French and 7,000 mounted men had already outflanked the Boers further to the west.

How did the men feel about the officers who carried out Hamilton's suicidal orders? In February 1989 I think that I found the answer in the small military cemetery at Maraisburg, Roodepoort. The grave of Captain St John Meyrick, the only Gordon Highlander officer killed at Doornkop, has this inscription:

"Well done good and faithful servant, enter thou into the joy of thy Lord. Matthew 26 v 23". However, this is a misquote, as the text is actually taken from Matthew 25 verse 23. The text for Matthew 26 verse 23 quoted on the grave reads: "And He answered and said, he that dippeth his hand with Me in the dish, the same shall betray Me". I leave it for others to judge whether this was a deliberate misquote—the numbers on the headstone are clear and indisputable.

Captain Meyrick's headstone in Maraisburg cemetery, Roodepoort, with the incorrect Biblical reference.

As Lord Roberts's protégé, Ian Hamilton continued with his successful military career into the First World War, when Churchill shifted the blame for the failure of the Dardanelles campaign onto Hamilton. An echo from Colenso perhaps, but with different players—sold by a politician? He died as recently as 12th October 1947 at his home, No.1 Hyde Park Gardens, London. He was buried beside his wife at Doune, in the very heart of Scotland. (Hamilton, 1966, p.456).

Ill-prepared

When General Buller was sent out as Commander-in-Chief to South Africa, he received no letter of general instructions from the government, neither prior to his departure, nor after his arrival. Furthermore, in the months leading up to the declaration of war, no Council of War was held, and Buller was never summonsed before the Defence Committee, nor invited to attend the Army Board meetings at the War Office. (Coetzer, 1996, pp.104 – 105). He had no instructions, and no plans of campaign had been discussed.

When Lord Roberts took over as Commander-in-Chief in South Africa, he pointed out to the Secretary of State for War that not a single commander in South Africa (including Buller) had ever had an independent command in the field. (Griffith, 1974, p.202).

Despite the existence of a general outline of defence, which included the holding of Ladysmith, no attempt was ever made to do a reconnaissance of the Ladysmith area. General Hunter gave evidence to the Commission of Inquiry after the war, stating that only one officer had ever been to the top of Bulwana Hill—the most dominant geographical feature—that was later occupied by the besieging Boer forces. (Coetzer, 1996, p.58).

Inaccessible treasure

The manifest of a train ambushed near Balfour showed that £60,000 were in a safe in the rear compartment. With no explosives left, the Boers tried firing into the lock, to no avail (Uys, 1981, p.74).

At the outbreak of war Org Meyer of the Heidelberg District buried £16,000 worth of gold sovereigns on his farm Meyersplaas. When he returned after the war he found that local treasure hunters had dug many holes. To stop further digging, he made a treasure hunter watch him dig up the coins. (Uys, 1981, p.232).

Incomplete burial

When Lieutenant Fuller visited the Modder River battlefield some time after the battle to find the grave of a brother subaltern, he found the bones of one of the dead man's feet sticking out, and buried them as best he could. (Fuller, 1981, p.128).

J

Jewish courage

A Jew named Kaplan fought courageously for the Boers. On one occasion he crept up to a blockhouse with two bombs slung around his neck in a saddlebag. During the Boer sporting contest at Pilgrims Rest on 17th December 1901, with his astute business sense, he took on the role of bookmaker during the horseracing. (Schikkerling, 1964, p.338).

Just desserts

Lieutenant Pohlman of the Johannesburg Police was one of the two officers under Veld-kornet Emmett, who went across the river at Colenso to capture Long's guns. (Coetzer, 1996, p.92). Badly wounded by shellfire, he was taken prisoner at Bergendal after the 100-gun bombardment. (Jones, 1999, p.17).

K

Keeping informed

It seems that the British made up for their lack of military intelligence by reading the newspapers. Opinion in the Boer lines at Colenso was that Hlangwane Hill was the key to their position, and the relief of Ladysmith. This was published in the French newspaper *Le Matin* early in February 1900. Later that month Buller attacked that position, and succeeded in his fourth attempt to relieve Ladysmith. This caused General Botha to write a letter to the Boer press, warning the newspapers to be more cautious in their reports. (Coetzer, 1996, p.95).

Kindness to the enemy

A British doctor was attending to a burgher who had received a bayonet wound at Monte Cristo, when his assailant walked past and recognized him. 'Is he bad, sir?' the soldier asked. 'Yes, pretty bad,' came the reply. 'Well, I did it as gently as I could. Fact, it wasn't so much the shoving of it in as the drawing of it out that hurt him!' said the Cockney. 'Then I gave him a drink out of my canteen when I was done with him. I think it was a bit of luck for him to have met me, don't you?' (Macdonald, 1999, p.285).

Two commandos surprised and badly wounded an English officer near Heidelberg. They then dressed his wounds and took him into the nearest British camp. Their act of humanity was so appreciated that they were given supper and a bath before leaving the camp. After the war the officer's parents visited one of the commandos, Leonard Buys, to thank him for saving their son's life. (Uys, 1981, p.169).

Lord Methuen was the only British General to be captured by the Boers in reasonable shape. (The mortally wounded Major-General Penn Symons was a temporary Boer captive in Dundee, until he

"The last drop"—a contemporary re-enactment of a British soldier giving the last dregs from his water bottle to his dying comrade.

died). He was wounded in the thigh at Tweebosch and was captured by General Delarey, who in spite of the protests from his commandos sent him to the British hospital at Klerksdorp. After the war they became friends, and when Methuen heard of Delarey's death in 1915 he said: 'I have lost a brave enemy in war, and a true friend in peace.' (Orford, 1971, pp.62, 64).

During the guerrilla phase of the war, the Boers left their serious casualties behind for the British ambulances. "Amid all the cruelty of farm burning and the hunting down of the civilian population, there was one redeeming feature, in that the English soldiers, both officers and men, were unfailingly humane. This was so well known that there was never any hesitation in abandoning a wounded man to the mercy of the troops, in the sure knowledge that he would be taken away and carefully nursed, a certainty which went so far to soften the asperities of the war". (Reitz, 1929, p.169).

Knowledge
At a farm near Krugerspost in September 1901, Schikkerling admired the wide variety of fruit trees in the orchard but remarked: 'Many surprises by the enemy were sprung upon our sentries in this garden before our arrival, so we concluded that the tree of knowledge grew not here.' (Schikkerling, 1964, p.304).

Krugersdorp statue
Even though President Kruger died in exile in Europe after the end of the war, his memory is still held in the highest regard by many South Africans. In October 1962, there was much consternation in the town when Laurika Postma's statue of Kruger was unveiled. The congregation of Kruger's Church, the Nederduitse Gereformeede Kerk ("Doppers") demanded to know why Kruger's statue was placed with its back to the Church. After some quick thinking, the Town Council explained that the orientation was deliberate as, "At least Kruger won't have to watch his back".

The statue of President Paul Kruger next to Paardekraal Drive, Krugersdorp. The church spire is in the background to the left.

L

Ladies of the night

In March 1902, a black woman called at the Fordsburg Commando, alleging that a burgher owed her a blanket for services rendered. The burgher was picked out at an identification parade, and the woman's husband, who was with her, remarked that she "often combined business with pleasure". (Schikkerling, 1964, p.369).

In Cape Town, the ladies of the night promoted business by having their names and addresses stamped on a bright metal disc, which looked like a sovereign. "They would walk about the streets smelling out their prey, and when they saw a likely catch would drop an address coin in front of him. I remember seeing a girl, perhaps unusually bold, walking through Green Point camp and throwing sovereigns' worth of trouble into the officers' tents". (Fuller, 1937, p.70).

In Pilgrims Rest the Chief's wife bartered her honour for safety matches, which were very scarce. "As her honour waned from full moon, so the tariff of eleven matches diminished, but never below a number that would at least yield warmth, if not fire". (Schikkerling, 1964, p.371).

Lady Roberts

One of the 4.7-inch naval guns was nicknamed "The Lady Roberts", after the Commander-in-Chief's wife. It was captured by the Boers at Helvetia, and General Ben Viljoen wrote a letter to General Smith-Dorrien as follows: 'I have been obliged to expel The Lady Roberts from Helvetia, this lady being an undesirable inhabitant of that place. I am glad to inform you that she seems quite at home in her new surroundings, and pleased with the change of company". General Smith-Dorrien replied: "As the lady referred to is not accustomed to sleep in the open air, I would recommend you to try flannel next to the skin". (Viljoen, 1903, p.179).

Last casualties

On 9th March 1953, more than 30 children and a school teacher were injured at the Crosby Afrikaans-medium school after a pupil (Jacobus Jordaan) accidentally dropped a three-pound British shell dated 1901, which he had found on a nearby koppie. (Lee, 1985, pp.1 – 2). It is unlikely that these will end up being the last Anglo Boer War casualties as there are still many unexploded shells waiting to be unearthed. In 1981 I took a live pom-pom shell, found in a vlei near Dullstroom, to the Military History Museum in Johannesburg for positive identification. The munitions expert refused even to come near it, and I took it back to its discoverer in Dullstroom, where it is displayed with pride above the fireplace.

The last casualty at Spion Kop was Wynand Els of the Pretoria Commando, on the day after the battle. While looting from a dead British soldier, he grabbed his rifle by its barrel and it discharged, fatally wounding him in the stomach. The soldier died with his finger still on the trigger. (Uys, 1981, p.25; Ransford, 1967, p.115).

Last words

During the defence of Wagon Hill, Lord Ava put his head over a rock to fire at a Boer when he was hit. As he fell he exclaimed, 'Done!' (MacDonald, 1999, p.155).

Although this pre-dates the Anglo Boer War, I cannot resist including this reference to Matthew chapter 25, verse 23, which is a common inscription on many British War Graves. The grave of Captain Butler in the military cemetery at Calcutta has this inscription: "In memory of Captain James Butler, Royal Dublin Fusiliers, who was accidentally shot by his batman. *Well done good and faithful servant*".

In a voice trembling with emotion Sir George White addressed the people after the relief of Ladysmith: 'I thank you men, one and all, from the bottom of my heart, for the help and support you have given to me, and I shall always acknowledge it to the end of my life. It grieved me to have to cut your rations, but I promise you that I will not do it again. I thank God we have kept the flag flying.' (Griffith, 1974, p.362).

Schikkerling, a Boer commando, observed that the three words most commonly uttered by dying men are "Mother", "God", and "water". (Schikkerling, 1964, p.73).

Just after 11 am on 31st May 1902, the war ended with the signing of the Treaty of Vereeniging. Lord Kitchener then shook hands with each Boer present saying, 'We are all good friends now.' (Rosenthal, 1975, pp.1, 104). During this centenary I have visited towns and museums in all parts of this wonderful country and, in Afrikaans and English, this is the most frequent comment written in the Visitors' Books. In the exclusively British military cemetery

Melrose House, Pretoria, where the Peace Treaty of Vereeniging was signed on Saturday 31st May 1902.

at Sannah's Post, as a tribute to former enemies, the local Afrikaans schoolchildren have placed pebbles with their names and sometimes messages on the graves of British soldiers. Every grave had a flower on it. The capacity for forgiveness in South Africa never ceases to amaze me.

After the Heidelberg Commando had surrendered its arms on 5th June 1902, General Alberts ended his speech by quoting from Matthew chapter 25, verse 23: "His Lord said unto him, well done, good and faithful servant; thou hast been faithful over a few things, I will make thee ruler over many things: enter thou into the joy of thy Lord". (Uys, 1981, p.227).

On 2nd June 1908 General Buller died. His last words were: 'I am dying. Well, I think it is about time to go to bed now.' (Griffith, 1974, p.375).

Lightning
Anyone who has been caught out in the open veld during a typical

The grave of Private Pople in Machadodorp cemetery. Although he died during the British occupation after the war, he was one of the many soldiers killed by lightning.

South African electric storm can testify to the fear and sense of helplessness experienced by the British soldiers. Many British war graves bear the inscription "Killed by lightning". It would be interesting to find out how many of the 798 "accidental" deaths were caused by this phenomenon. In a letter to my father, in 1965, my great-uncle, a young gunner in the Royal Field Artillery during the Anglo-Boer War, wrote; "Christmas Eve 1901 all night march, at daybreak an artillery ambush. All the gunners and drivers were killed and, on the way to outspan, a flash of lightning killed seven of the Inniskilling Dragoons. Happened near Tafel Kop, between Standerton and Heilbron, not a great distance from Johannesburg". Uncle Archie's memory was commendably accurate 64 years after this incident. Creswicke reports that the ambush and lightning strike took place on the night of 19th / 20th December 1901. However he wrote that only three Dragoons were killed by lightning. (Creswicke, vol 7, 1902 p.160).

Private Edmunds, the great-grandfather of my publisher and friend, Chris Cocks, had a series of miraculous escapes but

The cupola of the Magistrate's Court, Krugersdorp, where a British sentry was struck by lightning.

lightning nearly got him in the end. A Mauser bullet hit him squarely in the chest and passed through his lungs. Another Mauser bullet hit just below the first, raked his body, and came out in the thigh without breaking a bone. Whilst lying almost pulseless for a number of days, he contracted pleurisy. Almost recovered in the hospital tent, and lying with his hand resting on the tent pole, he was struck by lightning and was nearly killed by the shock. (Macdonald, 1999, p.147).

On 11th January 1901, "Kilmarnock House" was struck by lightning, and the sentry on guard at the Court House in the town (Krugersdorp) was sent spinning, fortunately only receiving a severe shaking. (Romer, 1908, p.119).

Locust-screen
Captain Reynolds and his column of the South African Constabulary moved from the Lace Mines towards Bothaville to surprise the Boer laager there. His initial success ended with failure when a group of Boers crossed the Valsch River and came up behind Reynolds, under cover of a cloud of locusts. (Fuller, 1937, p.163).

Lone sniper
After the Battle of Bergendal the Guards Brigade was ordered to advance and capture the towns of Waterval Boven (meaning "above the waterfall"), and Waterval Onder ("below the waterfall"). There was a steep mountain pass leading down to Waterval Onder and the Reverend Lowry explains what happened: "From even descending into that gorge the whole brigade of Guards was held back for four-and-twenty hours by a solitary invisible sniper, hidden, no one could find out where, in some secure crevice of the opposite cliff. One of our mounted officers riding down to take possession of the village was seriously wounded; and some of the scouts already there were compelled through the same course to keep under close shelter. So the naval guns, the field guns, and the pom-poms were each in turn called to the rescue, and gaily rained shot and shell for hours on every hump

and hollow of that opposite cliff, but all in vain; for after each thunderous discharge on our side, there came a responsive 'ping' from the valiant Mauser-man on the other side. Then the whole battalion of Scots Guards was invited to fire volley after volley in the same delightfully vague fashion, till it seemed as though no pinpoint or pimple on the far side of the gorge could possibly have failed to receive its own particular bullet; but what gave rise to no little surprise, nobody seemed one farthing the worse. Just as the sun set the last sound we heard was the parting 'ping' of Brother Invisible. So no man might descend into the depths that night, hotel or no hotel! Even at midnight we were startled out of our sleep by the quite unexpected boom of our big guns, which had, of course during daylight, been trained on a farmhouse lying far back from the precipice opposite to us, and were thus fired in the dead of night under the impression that the sniper, and perhaps his friends, were peacefully slumbering there. If so, the chances are he sniped no more". (Lowry, 1902, p.195).

The official records of the Guards Brigade records this incident less eloquently: "30/8/00. Brigade, with Henry's M.I., Field Co. R.E., naval 12-pounders, and one 5-inch gun marched for Waterval Onder at 9:30 am, preceded by French's cavalry. Boers

After the battle of Bergendal a lone Boer sniper, hidden on this cliff above Waterval Onder, held up the entire Guards Brigade for more than a day.

made off as soon as the force appeared, except for a few snipers, who remained on the hillsides overlooking the town, and who, in spite of a heavy artillery and pom-pom fire and volleys from two companies of the Scots Guards, maintained their position till dusk". (ORGB, 1904, p.181). It wasn't until 3 pm two days later that the British marched into Waterval Onder.

Perhaps it was the same sniper who in the South Eastern Transvaal, on 6th February 1901, held up a British column. Major Crum of the 1st King's Royal Rifles tells the story: "I was still sitting talking to Wills of the 18th Hussars, who had a troop dismounted in advance of my Company, when from a ridge about 1,000 yards off 'ping-pong!' and my grey pony shied off as a bullet hit the ground at his feet. Back we all got ignominiously to where my Company was, and from the cover returned the fire at 1,800 yards, but with no effect on the sportsman, who kept up his firing with quiet regularity. The pom-pom opened, then the Leicesters of the advance guard, and next two guns and two Maxims—all firing at this one Boer, who only occasionally showed his head. When there was a lull in our firing we heard the pick-pock of his Mauser, and a bullet close to someone was like a signal, a wasp's sting, for a renewed fusillade on our part. The climax was reached when the sportsman, standing boldly up, folded his arms and defied us while you could have counted 20". (Crum, 1903, p.122).

Lost treasure
Two Boers are thought to have stolen the British paymaster's gold from the guard's van of the train wrecked near Greylingstad on 13th February 1901. One was killed, and the other hid the gold in an antbear hole. When he returned to fetch the gold he could not find it and, in spite of many treasure hunts for nearly 100 years, it probably still remains undisturbed. (Uys, 1981, p.115).

Love letters
Someone sorting through the English Christmas mail taken from a sabotaged train, found a letter addressed by a titled Lady to an army officer in which she wished her lawful husband "in hell".

She mentioned that she had enclosed a cartridge belt embroidered with silk from her petticoat. (Schikkerling, 1964, p.159).

During the early part of the war a Boer woman wrote an encouraging letter to her husband on commando: "Remain and do your duty. I do not wish to see you until the English have been driven 30 miles into the blue plains [the sea]. I can always find another husband, but not another Transvaal. P.S. Do not forget to bring a rifle for little Jan and a tame Englishman for the kitchen". (Schikkerling, 1964, pp.311 – 312).

Lucky escapes
When General Viljoen was ambushed by the British near Lydenburg on 25th January 1902, he and his companions were fired on by about 50 rifles. Three bullets killed his horse, and a bullet passed through his clothing and pocket book, leaving him unscathed. (Schikkerling, 1964, p.348). Two years before, at the Battle of Vaalkrans, Viljoen had had a lucky escape when a shell burst overhead and four of his men were killed beside him, and his rifle was smashed. (Griffith, 1974, p.313).

During the Battle of Bergendal the Grenadier officers stationed at Monument Hill had just finished their breakfast and were strolling out of their mess, when a Boer shell exploded precisely where they had been sitting. (Lowry, 1902, p.191).

Another lucky escape happened when a shell struck the Ladysmith Town Hall. "The legs of the chair were cut from under him; the mess-tin from which he was breakfasting, was punctured; the man himself had not a scratch, and lost nothing but his appetite". (Macdonald, 1999, p.71).

On 11th January 1901, three shots were fired at Private Venn, "... one going through his helmet and another through his greatcoat, jacket and shirt sleeve without harming him". He must have led a charmed life, as at the Battle of Paardeberg the previous year, two bullets had passed through his clothing. (Fuller, 1937, pp.89 – 90).

During an abortive escape attempt by British prisoners of war from the cage outside Pretoria, the lights failed and shots were fired. "Kentish, who was playing chess, said that one of the bullets came in and took the head off his queen". (Crum, 1903, p.54).

Carbineer H. Watkins-Pitchford wrote to his wife from Ladysmith at the end of January 1900, and told her of a lucky escape". "The nearest shave I think I have seen is that of a dhoolie-bearer who has just come in with both his thighs scorched on the inside. He was stooping down cutting grass when a large shell passed between his legs and burst safely yards in front of him". (Griffith, 1974, p.235 – 236).

Lucky shots
During the Siege of Ladysmith an Indian who was bent over his cooking-pot was hit squarely in the centre of his face by a 15lb shell. "His head was not shattered—the forehead, chin, and ears were intact and perfect—but there was nothing but a clean-cut hole in between". (Macdonald, 1999, p.85).

Colonel Dick-Cunyngham V.C. was killed by an almost-spent bullet when crossing a bridge a mile and a half away from the fight at Caesar's Camp, Ladysmith. (Macdonald, 1999, p.85).

After a fight at Grootvlei (South Rand Mine) on 26th December 1900, Andries Beytel of the Heidelberg Commando knelt down to drink at Commandant Buys's Leeuspruit farm dam. With a high ridge between himself and the enemy, Andries was relaxed. As he stood up, he was hit by a stray bullet in the chest, which killed him. (Uys, 1981, p.94).

A Boer commando fired at Lieutenant Fuller and his Black National Scouts near Doornkraal, and being outnumbered, Fuller retreated behind a hill. When they were a mile away from the Boers, a scout called Long Boy fired a single shot into the air. After the war Fuller was chatting to some ex-commandos in the bar at the Grand Hotel in Kroonstad. It turned out that one of the

Boers had taken part in the skirmish and he said: 'We fired several shots and only one was returned when the fugitives were out of sight, but would you believe it—it struck the heel of my left boot!' (Fuller, 1937, p.285).

M

Masquerade

General Ben Viljoen, suspecting that some Boer refugees living in the ruined church at Dullstroom were passing information to the British, sent two of his men in British officers' uniforms to interview them. "Roksak" Redelinghuis posed as Colonel Bullock and Bester, one of the General's staff, posed as Colonel Blood. The suspects handed over their cattle and valuables for safekeeping to the "English officers", and promised to give them information about Boer commando movements the next day. However, they were surprised the next morning when a Boer commando arrived to arrest them. On 13th July 1901, three of them, including the two Steenkamps, were tried and sentenced to three months' hard labour, and their property confiscated. The prisoners later escaped during a British attack on the Boer laager on 29th July 1901. (Schikkerling, 1964, pp.245, 252, 278).

The church in Dullstroom (now restored) where "Roksak" Redelinghuis posed as Colonel Bullock to expose Boer traitors living in the ruins.

The Boers loved to stage concerts and plays, and in September 1901 at Pilgrims Rest, staged a comedy around the incident of trapping the Steenkamps in the church at Dullstroom. General Viljoen and Roland Schikkerling took part as the two condemned men, together with some young women from the town. "At the leave-taking scene between the condemned men and their wives, prolonged kissing took place, longer than was set down in the part". (Schikkerling, 1964, pp.310 – 311).

Matters medical

The Boers were often accused of firing on medical personnel. In their defence the British surgeon, Blake-Knox, noted that the Red Cross badge had a diameter of only an inch and a half, and could not reasonably be seen at a distance by the enemy. (Coetzer, 1996, p.134).

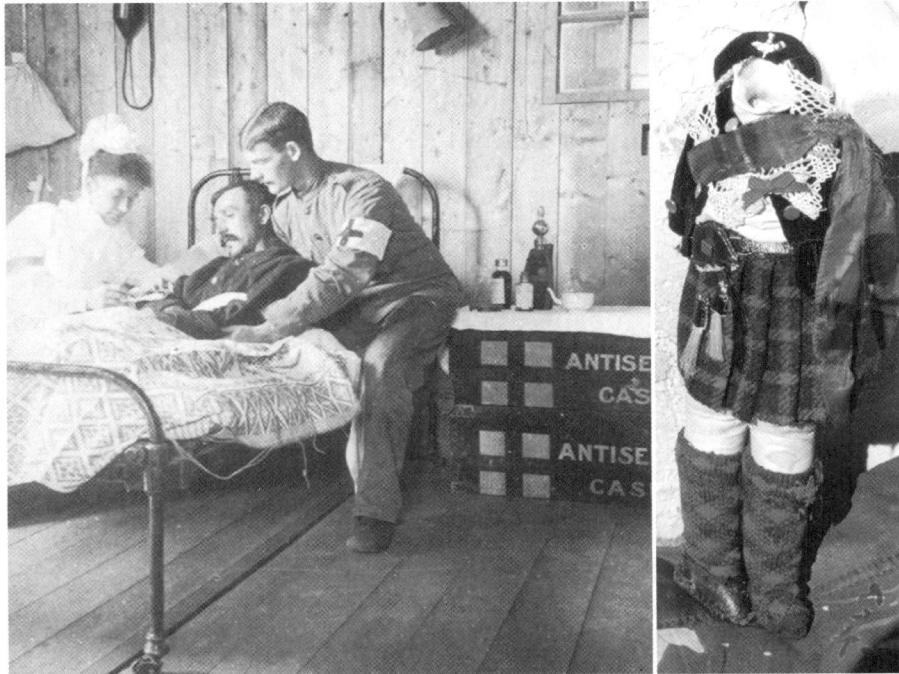

Left: In this posed contemporary photograph a mortally wounded British soldier dictates his last letter home. Right: Shirley Stone's doll (sans head) made from a piece of kilt. This was a gift to her grandmother in return for nursing a Scottish soldier at Burgersdorp.

It is reported that the first skin graft took place in Ladysmith during the Siege (although I have not been able to substantiate this). A young British soldier presented with a bad head wound and the surgeon had the local blacksmith fashion a metal plate to cover his shattered skull. The surgeon removed skin from his upper leg and sewed it into place over the plate. Apparently the soldier lived to a ripe old age and led a normal life. However, he could not go out into the sun for long!

Shirley Stone's grandmother was a nurse at the small British military hospital at Burgersdorp in the Cape. One of her patients was a Scottish soldier, and when he was invalided home he said that he had nothing to give her except a piece of his kilt. She had a doll made and dressed with the piece of kilt, and Shirley still has the doll.

A volunteer for the Imperial Yeomanry was rejected on the grounds that he had bad teeth. He responded by protesting that he wanted to fight the Boers, not eat them. (Cassell, 1903, p.352).

During the night attack on the Long Tom at Ladysmith a Guide, called Godson, was wounded by a shotgun loaded with steel ball bearings. Macdonald remarked; "Godson still has some of them in his leg, and is probably the only man in the British Empire going about on ball-bearings". (Macdonald, 1999, p.108).

Military advice
His Hottentot servant "Mooiroos" (Pretty Rose), who was a dedicated dagga smoker, attended to Commandant (later General) Ben Viljoen during many of his battles. After the Battle of Donkerhoek, Mooiroos observed that "... defeat was due to disregard of his advice as to the manner of the defence, the neglect of opportunities that had presented themselves, and, lastly, to the cowardice of a few officers". Schikkerling noted that there was much truth in his observations, and that Mooiroos would not have made a bad commander. (Schikkerling, 1964, p.22).

Mistaken identity

Lieutenant Fuller crept up on a Boer who was on sentry duty. At the 'Hands up!' command the boy jumped up, but still seemed to be no taller. He was a humpbacked dwarf, and Fuller burst out laughing. After disarming him, he demanded to know his name, which he gave as Christiaan de Wet. Thinking that he was pulling his leg Fuller said, 'Rot! What is your proper name?' 'Christiaan de Wet,' he replied, 'but I'm not the Christiaan de Wet!' (Fuller, 1937, p.232).

Mixed loyalties

A captain told his group of Black National Scouts that they could have their pleasure, if they wished, with their female Boer captives. Botha, a National Scout fighting with them, intervened and protected the women every night until they were handed over to the authorities. There is a Trooper Botha (most likely the same man) of the "Canadian Scouts" who is buried in the Kloof cemetery in Heidelberg. (Uys, 1981, p.167).

The grave of Trooper Botha, Canadian Scouts, in the Kloof cemetery, Heidelberg.

Money

On 12th May 1900, Veld-kornet Eloff attacked the besieged Mafeking garrison before sunrise through a gap between two small forts, "Hidden Hollow" and "Limestone Fort". After initial success, when they captured the old BSA barracks, fewer than 800 yards from Baden-Powell's headquarters, the British counter-attacked. A group of Eloff's men had taken refuge in a stone kraal, which was rushed by the British. One Boer hoisted a white flag, then threw it down and opened fire. A soldier saw him and rushed at him with bayonet fixed. The Boer yelled, 'Moenie, Moenie!' (Don't, Don't!). The Tommy paused, and then ran him through, shouting out, 'It's not your damned money, it's your bloody life I want!' (Fuller, 1937, pp.68 – 69).

Monuments

During the retreat from Natal, the Boers prepared a defensive position at Laings Nek, near Majuba. "In the succeeding days we dug trenches, scouted, mounted guard, blew in the tunnel, and generally augmented the historic interest of the place". (Schikkerling, 1964, p.16). The Rifle Brigade later helped the Royal Engineers repair the Laing's Nek tunnel, which took them six days. (Tucker, 1980, pp.112 – 113).

The British systematically destroyed many of the Boer Monuments as they occupied the towns. Examples are at Dullstroom, Belfast, and the stones that were removed from the Paardekraal Monument in Krugersdorp. The Dullstroom and Belfast Monuments have since been repaired, but the cairn of stones removed from the Paardekraal Monument was dumped into the Vaal River.

"Moses" stories

A Boer woman was forcibly removed from her farm and taken to a Concentration Camp and despite her protests, which were most likely not understood by the English-speaking troops, her seven year-old son and her baby were left in the farmhouse. For over a week her seven year-old son cared for the baby, giving it goat's milk and mealie-meal porridge. (Schikkerling, 1964 pp.266 – 267).

When the Boers first entered Natal, a lot of Indians fled in panic. Sannie de Jager found an Indian baby on the banks of a river, abandoned by its parents. She cared for and reared the child who later became her maid. (Schikkerling, 1964, p.267).

Music

Lieutenant-Colonel Grant, who had a musical ear, made an interesting observation about the noise of battle: "I became aware that the note permeating a battle is one endless E flat ... dropping occasionally a third of a tone, but always re-ascending to its endless semibreve". (Griffith, 1974, p.256).

Finding a smashed organ at a deserted farmhouse, a commando decided to use it as fuel. 'I placed a kettle on the flaming flats and sharps of the organ, and it soon sang.' (Schikkerling, 1964, p.213).

Farm burning was sometimes an occasion for music "We sat down and had a nice song round the piano. Then we just piled up the furniture and set fire to the farm". (Pakenham, 1997, p.438).

A war correspondent captured by the Boers, George Lynch, was much impressed by the Boers' hymn singing. "The chant rose and fell with a swinging solemnity. There was little of pleading or supplication in its tones; they were calling on the God of Battles; the God of the Old Testament was He to whom they sang rather than the Preacher of the Sermon on the Mount; and sometimes there was a strain of almost stern demand about it that gave it more the ring of a war-song than a prayer. Entering the door of that tent seemed like going into another century". (Griffith, 1974, p.157).

The Rifle Brigade marched in short, jaunty steps to the tune of *Ninety-five*, whilst the King's Royal Rifles marched sedately to the *Huntsman's Chorus*. If a soldier was dishonourably discharged and "drummed out" of the army the band played the *Rogue's March*. (Tucker, 1980, pp.133 – 134).

During the Boers' retreat from Waterval Boven to Nelspruit, after the Battle of Bergendal, a ganger's lorry came racing past Schikkerling's Commando. "A little while after, a ganger's lorry on which were a few of our companions with a piano which one was playing loudly, passed us running swift and free. We watched until the strains of the *Blue Danube* could be heard no longer". (Schikkerling, 1964, p.55).

The Black sentries used by the British along the railway line were taught to whistle. "I was further instructed by some genius of a staff officer that countersigns were not to be used, as Blacks could not understand them, and that a bar of some popular melody was to be whistled instead, each Black of course receiving musical instruction before proceeding on duty". (Fuller, 1937, p.115).

The ganger's lorry raced through this old ZASM tunnel near Waterval Boven, accompanied by a pianist playing the Blue Danube.

N

Natural interventions

The Devon Regiment arrived at about 3:30 pm on 6th January 1900, to reinforce the desperate garrison on Wagon Hill. The fate of Ladysmith hung in the balance as the Boers had a foothold on the hill, and could not be dislodged, in spite of a number of suicidal bayonet charges ordered by Ian Hamilton. At this point even Hamilton had had enough of blood-letting, but Sir George White overruled him and ordered the Devons under Colonel Park to storm the Boer positions. As they were preparing themselves, at 5 pm, a terrific thunderstorm broke out. At the height of the storm, with hail pelting down, the Devons charged and swept the Boers off the hill. This was totally unexpected, and the Devons were amongst them with the bayonet before they could react effectively. (Griffith, 1974, pp.220 – 222). Thus it can be said that a thunderstorm helped to save Ladysmith.

Naval warfare

Both of the Republics were landlocked and had no need of their own navies. At the beginning of the war Dr Leyds, the Transvaal Republic's representative in Europe, contracted a ship in Las Palmas to serve as a commerce-raider. However, the Republic failed to pay up, and the ship sailed on to other destinations in South America. (Rosenthal 1975, pp.1, 121).

An Italian ex-Naval officer, a foreign volunteer, failed to convince the Boer Presidents to adopt a visionary naval strategy. He proposed that three or four of the newly-invented submarines be acquired and based in German territory on the west coast to attack British troop transports and merchant ships. (Rosenthal 1975, pp.1, 121 – 122).

In January 1901, some burghers from General Hertzog's Commando reached Lambert's Bay on the Northern Cape coast.

They fired on a British warship anchored there, the *HMS Sybille*, but retreated behind the sand dunes when fire was returned. So ended the shortest, and only, naval engagement of the war. (Jones, 1999, p.132).

The Transvaal Republic was forced to start its own merchant navy in 1900, with the acquisition of the steamship *Rousillon*. The *Gironde,* which was contracted to run contraband military supplies through the British blockade to Mozambique, had suffered a unique breakdown. However, the *Rousillon* never left the Mozambique port of Lourenco Marques, as the crew was too frightened of the British Navy. (Rosenthal 1975, pp.119 – 120).

When the sailors ran out of ammunition for their 4.7-inch naval guns, they were put on temporary latrine duty. They appropriately named the two latrine carts after their ships, *The Powerful* and *The Terrible*.

The small harbour at Lambert's Bay, Western Cape coast.

Near-fatal assumption

A young Boer received a terrible fright during his first skirmish and, imagining that he was wounded, raced up to his Veld-kornet and asked him what blood smelt like. 'Like dung!' screamed the exasperated officer. 'Then, Veld-kornet, I am mortally wounded!' (Schikkerling, 1964, p.301).

Nicknames

General Buller, infamous for his vacillation and numerous defeats, was called "Sir Reverse", "The Ferry-man" (because he crossed the Tugela river so many times), "General Debility", and "General Paralysis". (Griffith, 1974, p.319).

"Roksak" Redelinghuis acquired his nickname (dress pocket), because he always carried one of his wife's dresses with him. This served as a constant reminder of his wife, and on one occasion helped to save his life. Badly wounded, and touching the dress he remarked: 'If I die the general will take my fair-haired wife.' (Schikkerling, 1964, p.245).

Major-General W. G. Knox was known as "Nasty Knox", because he had "a will of his own". (Fuller, 1937, p.149). Reverend Kestell reports how nasty he was to the Boers. On 27th January 1902, he removed Commandant Koen's wife from her house and had one of his colonels cross-examine her like a criminal. "This officer told her that her husband had captured 18 of his Blacks the day before, and said that if her husband had those Blacks shot, he, the colonel, would give the 1,000 Blacks under his command liberty to do with her as they chose". (Kestell, 1976, p.247).

Fighting-General Sarel Oosthuizen was known as "Rooi Sarel" (Red Sarel) because of the colour of his beard.

Colonel Baden-Powell was called "bathing-towel" by his men, as he often appeared dressed only in a towel after his baths in the field. (Lee, 1985, pp.52 – 63).

The Boer Long Tom on Bulwana Hill was damaged by a British shell near the end of the barrel, and sent to Pretoria for repairs. A section of the barrel was sawn off, and afterwards the gun was known to the Boers as "The Jew".

Long Tom replica, Ladysmith.

Captain Reginald Stephens, of the Rifle Brigade, was called the "Stiff'un" by his fellow officers; it is perhaps prudent not to find out why. (Bryant, 1972, p.191).

General Warren's nickname was "Jerusalem" Warren owing to his valuable contribution in the field of archaeology in Jerusalem during 1867 to 1870. (Coetzer, 1996, p.109).

Captain Congreve VC was called "Squibby" after the Congreve rocket, which his great-grandfather had invented. (Hall 1, 1999, p.106).

The Boer gun on Lombards Kop was appropriately given the nickname of "The Franchise" by the Boers, because the difficult citizenship rules, put in the way of foreigners by the Transvaal

Government, was a major cause of the war. Colonel Erasmus of the Staats Artillery told a war correspondent that any foreigner who wanted The Franchise could get it for nothing. (Macdonald, 1999, p.20).

The South African Imperial Light Horse was known to the Zulus as the "Sakkabulu Boys". (Griffith, 1974, p.293). This was a mark of respect for their fighting abilities because, when a bull (bulu) charges you, you kneel down (sak).

General Hart was known as "No Bobs Hart" because he refused to duck or bob under fire. (Griffith, 1974, p.30).

General Gatacre,after subjecting his men to long marches, was called "Backacre". (Pakenham, 1997, p.574).

One Tree Hill, across the Tugela from Spion Kop was renamed "Maconochie Hill" because Maconochie army rations were so frequently issued there. (Tucker, 1980, p.48).

For his ability to elude British columns on "De Wet hunts", General de Wet was attributed with magical powers and was called "De Wet O' De Wisp" by Punch magazine. (Tucker, 1980, p.144).

General Kitchener was called "Kitchener of Chaos", (K of K) because he had centralized the once-efficient regimental transport system and turned it into chaos.

The actual name of a major in the Malta Mounted Infantry was Pine Coffin. Would you serve under him? (Jones, 1999, p.277).

Throughout the war the heavy guns were known as "cow guns". They acquired this nickname at the beginning of the war when each British 4.7-inch naval gun had to be drawn by a span of 30 oxen. (Guest, 1902, p.45).

Nicotine
By August 1901, the Boer smokers were desperate for tobacco.

One Boer, Venter, had six inches of roll tobacco hidden in his saddlebag, and Dick Hunt, an American, caught him hiding behind his horse and biting off a quid. The angry American admonished him for not sharing, saying; 'You are lower than a snake's backside and I would not spit on you if your guts caught fire.' (Schikkerling, 1964, p.282).

Whilst a burgher was engaged in conversation he casually pulled a small Bible from his pocket, out of which he tore a page from the Book of Revelation, and proceeded to roll a cigarette. He remarked: 'I do not know how to accept the Revelation!' (Schikkerling, 1964, p.155).

General Hendrik Schoeman was the Boer commander opposing the British at Colesburg. One day a 4.7-inch lyddite shell landed outside his tent but failed to explode. He kept the shell as a souvenir and, when the Boer forces retreated, took it with him to his house in Pretoria and used it as an ashtray. Realizing the futility of carrying on the war when the British captured Pretoria, he took it upon himself to visit the commandos still in the field to try to persuade them to lay down their arms. He was imprisoned by the Boers, tried and sentenced to death.

Grave of General Schoeman and his wife and daughter in Hero's Acre, Pretoria.

Whilst he was awaiting execution in Barberton jail, the town was captured by the British and he was freed. Undeterred, he went on another mission and was re-arrested. Awaiting execution in Pietersburg jail, he was again freed by the British and returned to his home in Pretoria. Every Sunday evening he held a piano concert at his town house in Pretoria for his friends, who included British officers. On Sunday 26th May 1901, when he knocked his pipe out in the top of the lyddite shell it exploded, killing him, a friend, and his daughter.

This was a strange incident, reeking of sabotage. General Schoeman was familiar with explosives, having built a number of dams on his farm. His military experience would have ensured that he remove the lyddite from the shell before using it as an ashtray for nearly two months. It is possible that a *bittereinder* planted explosives in the shell on that fateful day.

Memorial to General Schoeman at Saartjies Nek, near Hartebeestpoort Dam.

His son erected a memorial to him on the top of a prominent hill at Saartjies Nek near Hartebeestpoort Dam, where the family farm used to be. In his book about his father he described him as: "... one of the great (perhaps the words 'highly principled' are more appropriate) sons of the South African Republic". (Schoeman, 1950, p.215).

Captain Naude, on the other hand, had this to say about Schoeman: "In the whole Boer Army there was surely no less-capable officer. After Colesburg was besieged he nestled with his commando in the hills as if he was glued there. He simply let

the chance to advance further south slip through his fingers".
(Scholtz, 1940, p.32).

The inscription on the memorial reads:

> Melancholy is the path of the peacemaker:
> Remember Hess...
> Remember Pétain...

No escape

During the Battle of Belmont some of the Boers left their positions
to escape on horseback. Commandant Greyling shot their horses,
compelling them to re-occupy their places in the firing line. (Guest,
1902, p.14).

After the British had taken the Johannesburg Police positions at
Bergendal, one of the Boers tried to escape from under the noses of
the Rifle Brigade. "A solitary mounted Boer appeared from behind
the farm and, making a dash for the gate, turned left and rode

*The farmhouse at Bergendal taken from the Johannesburg Police position.
Sergeant Ellis of the Rifle Brigade brought down a fleeing Boer horseman who
emerged from behind the farmhouse just after the rocky outcrop was taken.*

across our front. Everyone had a shot at him and everyone missed except Sergeant Ellis, who knelt down and took a steady aim and brought down the horse; it looked a wonderful shot and possibly it was a lucky one. The rider was knocked out with his sudden fall and was easily added to the bag of prisoners". (Bryant, 1972, p.199).

General Viljoen was surprised to discover that the 2,000 British prisoners of war at Nooitgedacht were guarded by only 15 burghers armed with Martini-Henry rifles. There was also a great quantity of provisions, rifles and ammunition at the nearby railway station. Had the soldiers overpowered their guards they would have found themselves fully armed and provisioned and able to cut off the retreat of half the Boer Army from Bergendal. General Viljoen noted that "... save for Tommy being such a helpless individual when he has nobody to give him orders and to think for him, these 2,000 men might have become a great source of danger to us had they had the sense to disarm their 15 custodians (and what was there to prevent their doing so?) ..." (Viljoen, 1903, p.187).

The site of the British POW camp at Nooitgedacht, Elands River Valley.

No quarter

The Boers were incensed by the British use of locally recruited Black troops, as this was a "White Man's War". During the action at Klip River on 23rd November 1900, the Boers cornered a group of about 20 Black soldiers who were fleeing the battlefield, and wiped them out to a man. (Uys, 1981, p.84).

During the attack by General Smuts on Modderfontein Post, near Bank Station on 31st January 1901, Commandant Breytenbach was killed whilst attacking the small forts to the east of the British positions. On discovering that these positions were manned by Black troops, General Smuts attacked them, ruthlessly killing them all. (Uys, 1981, p.105).

The Boers raided a blockhouse near Heidelberg, which was garrisoned by Black National Scouts under the command of a European officer. The Boers lured away 13 Scouts, and only one got away. A few weeks later the blockhouse was again attacked and the scouts, their women, and officers, were virtually wiped out. The survivors were later tried by the Boers and shot. (Uys, 1981, p.172).

A British blockhouse at Harrismith.

No surrender

During the Battle of Spion Kop, some British troops in the main trench on the right threw down their arms and surrendered. As the Boers came forward to take their prisoners, Colonel Thorneycroft ran up to them and shouted; 'I'm the Commandant here; take your men back to hell, sir! I allow no surrenders.' He then took some of the men to a line of rocks behind the main trench and opened fire on the Boers, who managed to get away with a few prisoners. (Pakenham, 1997, p.298).

The forward Boer positions at Spion Kop looking towards the main British trench, which is marked by the memorials on the skyline.

O

Obedience

General Kitchener ordered a suicidal cavalry charge on the Boer camp at Paardeberg, a distance of 500 yards over open ground. Colonel Hannay, commanding the 1st Mounted Infantry Brigade, sent his officers away on various pretexts and then gathered 40 to 50 men together for the charge. Far in front of his men his horse was shot from under him, but he advanced on foot to within 200 yards of the laager where he fell, riddled with bullets. His Adjutant, Captain Hankey, and a few of the men were killed, but the others swerved to the left to safety. Two officers and a handful of men actually reached the laager and were taken prisoner. (Trew, 1999, p.154). Hannay gave his life to demonstrate that a cavalry charge was inappropriate in the circumstances.

O.K. Corral

During the battle for Wagon Point on 6th January 1900, a shoot-out reminiscent of the gunfight at the O.K. Corral took place between the opposing senior commanders. As Colonel Ian Hamilton and Major Miller-Wallnut of the Gordon Highlanders came up, the Boers renewed the attack and the British took flight. Six men, including Ian Hamilton, stood their ground and stopped the flight. Then there was a desperate race between the Boers and British for the gun pit. "What a lethal race! First was Hamilton, who leaned on the sandbag parapet and fired at the nearest Boer with his revolver. Trooper Albrecht fired. And then Lieutenant Digby Jones with a Corporal Hockaday, Royal Engineers, appeared, each firing at a Boer. Suddenly, almost everybody was shot. De Villiers, De Jager and Gert Wessels lay dead. Miller-Wallnutt got a bullet through the head and Trooper Albrecht fell a moment later. Lieutenant Digby Jones ordered some of his nerve-shattered men back to their positions and was then shot through the throat, and died. Lieutenant Dennis, Royal Engineers, ran to his side to help and was also shot. Colonel Ian Hamilton, who had braved other such hair-raising events on other occasions, miraculously stood unscathed. It is said, and it was the opinion of Colonel Hamilton (later, of course, to become General Sir Ian Hamilton) that De Villiers shot Miller-Wallnutt and Digby Jones shot De Villiers. Anyway, that courageous carnage seemed to settle Wagon Point and the charmed and charming Hamilton returned to the battle at Wagon Hill" (Griffith, 1974, p.220).

The "Lady Anne" gun pit at Wagon Point, Ladysmith, where the shoot-out took place. The memorial to Lt Digby Jones is visible in the background.

Opportunities lost

Just before Ladysmith was besieged, the British attacked the Boers at Nicholson's Nek. They were routed, and about 10,000 soldiers fled towards Ladysmith. The Boers had superior numbers and were mounted. While General Joubert hesitated, General Christiaan de Wet muttered to him 'Los jou ruiters; los jou ruiters!' (Release your horsemen!). Joubert held back and quoted a Dutch saying, 'When God holds out a finger, don't take the whole hand!' (Reitz, 1929, p.43 to 44). Veld-kornet Isaac Malherbe remarked: 'It might be sound theology, but it was no good in making war!' (Griffith, 1974, p.88). If he had let his commandos pursue the fleeing soldiers, Ladysmith would most likely have fallen that day, changing the course of the war.

The British repeated this mistake, after the relief of Ladysmith. Referring to the chaotic Boer retreat on 28th February 1900, General Lyttelton criticized Buller's inaction: "... dispirited by defeat, encumbered by a huge train of wagons, the Sundays River in flood behind them with only one bridge, they were at our mercy. Few commanders have so wantonly thrown away so great an opportunity". (Griffith, 1974, p.365). Surgeon Blake-Knox wrote: "Over Ladysmith floated a balloon. Had we known what its occupants saw, the Boer retreat might, by a combined advance of infantry, guns and mounted men, have been turned into a complete rout". (Coetzer, 1996, p.252).

When the Boers realized that General Yule and his column had left Dundee, they failed to follow them, being content to loot the British camp. They could have inflicted very heavy losses on the column during their four-day march—as it turned out, the 4,000 soldiers were an invaluable addition to the garrison of Ladysmith. (Griffith, 1974, pp.62 – 63).

It was impossible for General Botha to follow up his victory at Spion Kop by attacking the retreating enemy the next day. The commandos had fought continuously for eight days, and built trenches every night. At about nine o'clock on 24th January 1900, while firing still continued on the Kop, an officer found General Botha and his staff around the table in Major Wolmarans's tent, asleep from exhaustion. (Coetzer, 1996, p.158). For the next two days the Boer Army watched the British withdrawing across the Tugela, without firing a shot at them. As the engineers dismantled the last of the pontoon bridges Botha fired a single shell at them, which splashed into the Tugela. (Pakenham, 1997, p.306).

The memorials on the horizon mark the British trenches on Spion Kop, viewed from the Boer position on Green Hill.

Owning up

Major Erasmus of the State Artillery took the blame for the successful attack on his Long Tom gun outside Ladysmith. He even went so far as to ask the State Attorney to place him under arrest. (Griffith, 1974, p.153).

Colonel Bullock of the 2nd Devons took the blame for the loss of the 10 guns at Colenso. He had been protecting the guns with two sections of his men, and being so far forward, had not received Buller's orders to retire. Although he had refused to surrender when Veld-kornet Emmett approached to capture the guns, some of his men, desperate for water, raised the white flag. When he reached for his revolver one of the Boers clubbed him over the head with a rifle butt, stunning him. In the ambulance train he pinned a piece of paper to his breast reading; "I am the officer who lost 10 guns at Colenso". (Griffith, 1974, pp.192 – 193).

P

Peace

When an old Boer woman called Koekemoer was first told that peace had been made, she said to her informant: 'May your mouth turn into gold.' (Schikkerling, 1964, p.391).

Pets

The Rifle Brigade had a pet liver-and-white springer spaniel, which took part in their final charge during the Battle of Bergendal. "He was well in front with his tail in the air and his nose on the ground. He seemed excited and puzzled; this kind of a shoot was new to him. The little puffs of dust the bullets kicked up as they struck the ground around interested him enormously, and he kept running up to first one and then another, but he could not make them out. When we paused for breath in our rushes he ran up and down our line while we lay close to the

The view of the open ground over which the Rifle Brigade charged to take the Johannesburg Police position at Bergendal—a view from the Boer position.

ground, and before long he stopped a bullet just behind his left shoulder. We thought the old dog was done for, but after the first shock he recovered a bit and managed to drag himself after us and finally rejoined the company after the position was won". (Bryant, 1972, p.195).

General Kitchener rescued two baby starlings that had fallen down the chimney of his bedroom at GHQ in Pretoria. One died, but he put the other one in a cage and made his senior staff responsible for its wellbeing, much to their disgust. While he was on a visit to Pietersburg the bird escaped and, on his return, he mobilized a small army made up of his staff and personally supervised a hunt for the bird. It was eventually found in a neighbour's chimney and the Chief happily returned to Headquarters covered in mud, "having repeatedly fallen prone in wet flower beds". (Pakenham, 1997, p.539).

Picking up pebbles

In December 1880, the Transvaal burghers gathered at Krugersdorp and took a vow that they would fight for their freedom to the death, as a consequence of Britain annexing the Transvaal Republic in 1877. As a symbol of their vow, each burgher placed a stone on a cairn. The Transvalers subsequently won the First Anglo Boer War, and built the Paardekraal Monument over the cairn of stones. When the British captured Krugersdorp in 1900, they loaded all the stones from the cairn onto railway trucks and dumped them into the Vaal River. Nearly half a century later a package arrived from Lieutenant Colonel H.F.M. Jourdain C.M.G., which contained one of the stones. He explained that he had been on guard at the Paardekraal Monument when the stones were removed and that he had kept the stone as a souvenir, which he was now returning. (De Klerk, 1987, pp.10 – 11). Today the monument stands over the imaginary cairn of stones erected in 1880, and the single remaining stone is kept in a safe in Krugersdorp.

The Paardekraal Monument, Krugersdorp, built over the cairn of stones which was removed by the occupying British troops and thrown into the Vaal River.

Porridge

After Eloff's unsuccessful attack on Mafeking, he and his men were held captive in the prison. One of his commandants was given a bowl of thin porridge for his dinner—a luxury during the final days of the siege. "He looked at it, then at his hands, and taking it for soap and water proceeded to wash in it". (Fuller, 1937, p.69).

Pot plants

When farms were raided for supplies, some items were regarded as useful and others were not. "There is a quantity of mealie cobs in the wagon house, which the women allow us to take; and also a few pot plants that we allow them to keep". (Schikkerling, 1964, p.205).

Practical joke

The commandos camped outside the town of Pilgrims Rest used the narrow gauge miners' trolleys to race into town. Soon all the trolleys ended up in town, and a few Boers laboriously pushed a trolley uphill to their camp to ensure an easy ride into town the next day. Even though they took the trolley off the rails as a precaution, while they were sleeping some rascal, by way of a joke, rode it into town and wasted their hard labour. (Schikkerling, 1964, p.310).

Premonitions

Major Childe, who led the South African Light Horse in the attack on Bastion Hill before the battle at Spion Kop, had a premonition of his death the night before the battle. He requested his brother officers to put an epitaph above his grave quoting 2 Kings chapter 4, verse 26: "Is it well with the child? It is well". (Griffith, 1974, p.255). Childe died from a head wound, and his wish was granted. At his funeral service Lord Dundonald quoted from 2 Kings chapter 4, verse 19: "And he said unto his father, 'My head, my head,' and he said to a lad, 'Carry him to his mother.'" (Griffith, 1974, p.255).

Chris Muller explains in great detail how, from the beginning of guerrilla warfare, whenever the British came close, a muscle just above his knee began to "pull". The nearer the enemy came the more it pulled. When he was fighting, if the muscle began pulling from behind, the British retreated or disengaged. He found this strange, but the enemy never once surprised him. After the war, it never recurred. (Muller, 1936, p.42).

Prophecy

General Delarey was accompanied by the famous Boer prophet, "Siener" (Seer) van Rensburg, who had many visions, most of which were concerned with bulls or buck. Before the Battle of Tweebosch he had the following vision: "I see a red bull coming from the direction of Vryburg. His horns are pointing forwards. He is eager to fight. He is brave and strong but, when he arrives at Barberspan, his horns hang lower. His determination is failing and he begins to feel discouraged. But it will go even worse with him because, when he arrives at the Harts River, he will be completely dehorned. He will be unable to butt. He must be disarmed then". The Siener also saw the Boers walking about among the British guns and wagons. Inspired by this vision, on 7th March 1902, Delarey smashed up Lord Methuen's column of 1,200 men and four field guns, and captured Methuen. (Orford, 1971, p.61 to 62).

The day before the war ended with the Treaty of Vereeniging, General Hertzog said: 'We are nearer the time when a Great War must break out. It is a known fact that the nations are arming themselves more and more, and building ships of war, which is all done in preparation for the day when war will break out in Europe.' (Rosenthal, 1975, p.99).

Q

Queen's birthday

The British prisoners of war were determined that the Union Jack would fly over Pretoria on the Queen's birthday, 24th May 1900. 'The Union Jack floated over Pretoria that day, for Haserick let loose a tame hawk with the Union Jack tied to its neck, and sent it hovering over the town". (Crum, 1903, p.55).

Queen's touch

Queen Victoria gave Lieutenant Roberts's posthumous Victoria Cross to his mother in a sealed packet, saying: 'Do not open it until you get home; no other hands but mine have touched this.' (Griffith, 1974, p.202).

On 26th February 1900, the Queen's personal gift of chocolate arrived at the front lines of Buller's army that was about to relieve Ladysmith. With her own money she had bought a specially designed tin of chocolate for every British soldier serving in South Africa. (Griffith, 1974, p.342). Many British soldiers sent the tins back home intact for safekeeping, as the gift was so highly prized. Private Tucker chose to eat his chocolate. "The empty tin now became an object of interest, so I carefully wrapped it up and placed it in my haversack. I carried it during all the fighting my regiment was involved in until I had a chance to send it to England. I fear the box got a few knocks but it still remains the Queen's gift and much cherished". (Tucker, 1980, p.67).

R

Railway warfare

Cornered by the British Army at Hectorspruit, near the Portuguese border, the Boers destroyed the supplies and impedimenta that they were unable to carry north to the bushveld. Some men staged breakneck collisions between heavy goods trains, whilst others "... dynamited the bridges and then allowed locomotives at full speed to race to the river and throw themselves against the massive pillars in mid-stream and die down in the fizzling water and steam". (Schikkerling, 1964, p.68).

When Commandant Buys blew up the goods train six kilometres east of Greylingstad on 13th February 1901, he found that it was closely followed by an armoured train, which started firing its cannon at his commando. The goods train had its carriages in

Old ZASM railway bridge near Machadodorp.

front, so that if a charge blew up the tracks, the crew could uncouple the derailed trucks and steam off to safety. Buys's men raced to the train, uncoupled the engine, and engaged reverse gear, sending it racing at full steam towards the armoured train. "The armoured train was forced to steam backwards in order to avoid a collision. It was a race as far as we could see. I never discovered how far they travelled". (Uys, 1981, p.114).

Religious service

A Boer preacher and his congregation were fervently engaged in prayer when the preacher caught sight of approaching British horsemen from his superior vantage point. He leapt over his flock and onto his horse, before his congregation knew what was happening. A youth caught up to him in their wild flight and said; 'Dominee, you forgot to say Amen!' (Schikkerling, 1964, p.80 – 281).

Just before the relief of Ladysmith, on the night of Sunday 25th February 1900, the Rifle Brigade were moved by the singing of the 100th Psalm from the Boer lines. They even stood up to listen but, just before the Amen had finished, they received a heavy volley from the Boer trenches, which made them dive for cover. "Only a minute before we had been giving them credit for their religious ways and were even praising their singing and this was the way they returned our kindness for letting them have their service in peace!" (Tucker, 1980, p.74 to 75).

A padre approached the blockhouse line on his way from Vredefort, and asked whether he could hold a religious service there. This was to ease his conscience as he was hours late for a service at Headquarters. He insisted on holding the service inside the blockhouse, which had a standard door measuring only four-foot square. By the time the seven men and Lieutenant Fuller had crawled into the blockhouse they had developed the giggles. A sudden noise outside startled one of the men, who let off an "explosion". It drove the men out of the blockhouse in five seconds flat and, once in the fresh air, they all nearly died with laughter. Soon the padre joined in, and when he had regained his breath exclaimed: 'Well, well, well, with that man in your blockhouse you ought to be as safe as in the Tower of London!' He then produced a bottle of port and they had "tea" together. (Fuller, 1937, pp.132 – 133).

Inside the blockhouse at Harrismith, showing the four-foot square door.

Remains and controversies

Today the remains of an artillery emplacement can still be found on the top of Groot Zuikerboskop at Dullstroom, in original condition. Controversy still exists as to whether a Long Tom was positioned here during the Battle of Bergendal. Evidence from Schikkerling's diary indicates that it was. On 17th April 1901, Schikkerling's Commando was in position above O'Grady's farm at Elandshoek, on the road from Dullstroom to Lydenburg (Schikkerling, 1964, p.174), watching the enemy advance towards them from Belfast. "The enemy will probably place a gun in the same schantz on Suikerbosch Kop, in which Long Tom was placed during the Battle of Bergendal". (Schikkerling, 1964, p.175).

The remains of the artillery emplacement above Dullstroom.

Remembrance

On 7th November 1900, Commandant Hendrik Prinsloo was killed near Belfast, while leading the Carolina Commando on an attack on General Smith-Dorrien's column. He was one of the Boer heroes of the Battle of Spion Kop, and was shot dead within sight of his wife and family. He was buried on the battlefield, and every year on the anniversary of his death a few burghers gather together to stand in silence and tribute to "… one of the few men who took away from Spion Kop a better reputation then he had brought to it". (Ransford, 1969, p.133).

Reprisals

To discourage the sabotaging of railways, the British issued a proclamation that the farmhouse nearest to the damage would be razed. Thus Mr van Rensburg of the farm Houtpoort found himself standing with his wife and children in the veld, after his farm had been destroyed as a result of the train destroyed just south of Heidelberg on 2nd September 1900. (The high embankment where the train was wrecked can be seen next to

Commandant Prinsloo's memorial near Belfast erected with funds raised after the war by his adversary, General Smith-Dorrien.

the N3 Freeway between Johannesburg and Durban at the Balfour off-ramp). (Uys, 1981, p.70).

During the guerrilla phase of the war, the Boers were compelled to wear captured British uniforms, as this was their only source of clothing. The British issued a proclamation stating that any Boer captured in British uniform would be shot. Reitz maintains that neither the commandos nor the local population were informed that the death penalty attached to the wearing of British uniforms. In fact, many of Smuts's men who were taken prisoner were executed for wearing khaki, and his commando sincerely believed that the British had resorted to shooting prisoners. (Reitz, 1929, p.236).

Frans Kruger of the Heidelberg Commando captured a British uniform after the action at Dam Plaats (near Frankfort) on 25th January 1902. Although the commando had strict instructions to cut all military insignia off captured uniforms, Frans was too tired to do so, and was captured the next day. He was tried and found guilty of wearing a British uniform, and executed. (Uys, 1981, p.188).

Research in reverse

I found some of the stories related by Fuller in his book *The Last of the Gentleman's Wars* so capricious that I decided to do some research in reverse. On pages 90 – 91 he describes the death of Private Appleby in a typical night skirmish, and relates that he was subsequently buried at Heilbron. Sure enough, I found private Appleby's grave in the military section of the cemetery at Heilbron, and his date of death tallied with that in Fuller's diary.

The grave of Private Appelby in Heilbron cemetery.

Restraint

Although the British resorted to farm burning, the Boers showed restraint in not retaliating at the farmhouses of National Scouts. In November 1901, Schikkerling reported that the only house not burnt down near Pilgrims Rest was that of Harry Harber, who led a band of National Scouts. (Schikkerling, 1964, p.327).

Rock art

Bored soldiers on both sides spent many hours recording their presence on the rocks and boulders of lonely koppies. Petty Officer Franklin wrote in his diary on 28th November 1899: "I was cutting my name into a rock whilst the Fort was being shelled when one shell landed to the rear, striking the cookhouse..." "Sharp Eyes" Khaigan, a friend and fellow historian (aren't all historians friends?), found Franklin's name engraved on a rock at Caesar's Camp, Ladysmith, nearly 100 years later. To cap this he also found the cookhouse in the shelter of some boulders, suitably engraved with a fork and spoon, scattered with rock fragments from the exploded shell.

Petty Officer Franklin's engraving at Caesar's Camp, Ladysmith.

The site of the cookhouse in which the shell exploded. Caesar's Camp, Ladysmith.

S

Saluting the throne

Wherever he went a well-known officer (who must remain anonymous) carried with him a portable latrine, a seat and canvas folding screen. "During the battle [of Modder River] he had this pitched, and one morning as was his habit, he retired to it. As he was in his sanctum, a burial party consisting of a corporal and some half-dozen men of his unit marched by; whereupon a dust devil whirling over the veld neatly removed the canvas screen and carried it into the air. There was the great man enthroned. What could the corporal do? His duty of course; so he gave 'Eyes right!'" (Fuller, 1937, p.129).

Schoolboy warriors

A young wounded Boer named Schultz was brought into Ladysmith after the Battle of Wagon Hill, having just seen his father killed at his side. His only uniform was his hat, which had his Grey College (Bloemfontein) badge on it. (MacDonald, 1999, p.66).

On 2nd November 1901, President Steyn issued a proclamation lowering the age of compulsory military service to 14 years. (Kestell, 1976, p.216).

Sense of humour

President Kruger had a wonderful, but wicked, sense of humour, hard to imagine from his dour appearance and demeanour! He granted the Jewish community four stands in Johannesburg (free of charge) to establish a second synagogue and Jewish school. This was known as the Park Synagogue, situated on the corner of Joubert and De Villiers Streets. When Kruger arrived from Pretoria in September 1892 for the opening ceremony, he told his hosts that he come to convert the Jews. Legend has it that he then declared the synagogue open "...in the name of our Lord Jesus

Christ". However, it is more likely that this was the conclusion to his Christian grace, which he said at the banquet in his honour after the opening ceremony, much to the embarrassment of his hosts. (Kaplan, 1991, p.80 – 81).

General Botha had a great sense of humour, which prevented him from seeing the worst of the situation. "It kept his sympathies bright: and helped him to realize the other man's point of view. He lit the torch of racial toleration". (Chilvers, 1930, p.125). On one occasion, while travelling with General Smuts and Sir Thomas Cullinan near Tzaneen, an old farmer engaged them in conversation. He told them that now that the English were running the country, "We can't punish the natives. It's a pity. But I've found a way out. I just tie them up by the feet and tickle them very gently that way".

Long after this, Botha was being attacked in Parliament and he suddenly turned to Cullinan and said, 'These fellows deserve to be tied up by the feet and tickled a bit, don't they?' (Chilvers, 1930, p.124 – 125).

Botha maintained that his most humorous experience occurred near Heidelberg when the Boers were looting a British convoy. A serious old greybeard (who had never seen seafood) came up to Botha with an open tin of oysters and asked, 'Who will give me a tin of jam for this little tin of birds' stomachs?' (Chilvers, 1930, p.125).

Shaving

A Natal policeman was shaving on Christmas Day 1899, when a 90-pound shell fired at Ladysmith passed between the mirror and his face, stunning him. For the next hour he sat with his face in his hands mumbling, 'Not hurt; not hurt.' (Macdonald, 1999, p.40).

Preparing for a visit to a farm one evening, Schikkerling managed to shave one side of his face with a borrowed razor before it became hopelessly blunt. 'I posed side-faced all evening and, like the moon, showed always the same side of my face to the inhabitants of the earth.' (Schikkerling, 1964, p.200).

Signs in the sky
On the anniversary of the Transvaal's Independence Day, 16th December 1900, there was a total eclipse of the moon, which the besieged in Ladysmith interpreted as a sign for the eclipse of Boer independence. (Macdonald, 1999, p.126). Outside Ladysmith the relieving force was paraded at midnight but did not move out of Frere camp until 3.30 am, only to return to camp. Whilst waiting to move out of camp they amused themselves by watching an eclipse of the moon. (Tucker, 1980, p.36).

Towards the end of April 1901, a comet with a long tail appeared in the East. By early May, during the full moon, the comet appeared in the west and had two tails. Later in May the comet became faint and appeared in the north. (Schikkerling, 1964, pp.189, 194, 199). A Boer commando, Denys Reitz, observed that the comet was shaped like the letter "V". Seer Van Rensburg interpreted this as a sign of peace (the first letter in the word "vrede", which means peace), but the commandos jokingly said that it signified "vlug" (retreat). (Reitz, 1929, p.70). On the British side, Fuller noted that: "On May 2nd I first noticed a comet in the east; the next night, as I watched it, it seemed to me to have two tails. Then, on the 6th there was no doubt as to this; it had a short bright tail fanning out towards a bright star below Orion's Belt, and a long dim tail fanning out towards four stars which may have been the Southern Cross, though the sketch in my diary does not say so". (Fuller, 1937, p.97). It is interesting that Fuller did not try to attach any meaning to the appearance of the comet.

Shortly before peace was concluded, on the night of 22nd April 1902, there was a striking eclipse of the moon. (Schikkerling, 1964, p.381).

Silence
In numerous defensive battles the Boers held their fire as long as they could, and this had a profound psychological effect on their opponents. It was used to great effect at the battles of Modder River, Colenso, and the Tugela Heights. "One can imagine nothing more gloomy and terrible than this deathly silence of

British soldiers in a trench, awaiting a Boer attack.

crowded trenches and frowning gun-pits. Even on the imperturbable British private it is not altogether without its effect, and one may notice a corresponding silence—a bad sign with our soldiers in action—and uneasy glances at the hill-tops and ridges". (Griffith, 1974, p.309).

On 25th February 1900, after vicious fighting just before the relief of Ladysmith, a truce was concluded to enable the British to collect their wounded and bury their dead. Both sides were so moved by the scenes of suffering and slaughter that they had just witnessed, that they were unwilling to commence hostilities, which they, however, reluctantly resumed four hours after the end of the armistice. (Griffith, 1974, p.340).

Smokescreens

The Boers lit veld fires to conceal an attack, or to cover a retreat. On 25th May 1901, General Ben Viljoen attacked one of Plumer's convoys near the farm Mooifontein (between Bethal and Standerton), using a veld fire to cover their approach. However, after a running fight of some 14 kilometres, they were beaten off. (Uys, 1981, p.129; Jones, 1999, pp.153 – 154).

After the relief of Ladysmith the retreating Boers eluded their pursuers by means of smokescreens. "The foremost of our men had set fire in hundreds of places to the grass on either side of the road, and the smoke obscured many of us from the enemy. Had it not been for the smoke and the dust raised, we of the tail-end would have fared badly indeed". (Schikkerling, 1964, p.15).

The Earl of Dundonald, Commanding Officer of the Mounted Brigade, remembered his unusual inheritance while lying awake on the night after the Battle of Spion Kop, which had been covered in the smoke of exploding shells that day. His grandfather, Admiral Lord Dundonald, had conceived the idea of using smokescreens to cover naval attacks. He decided that the secret would be passed on to succeeding generations and would only be revealed in the event of a national emergency. Colonel Dundonald disclosed his secret to the War Office during the First World War, and the smokescreens were successfully used for the fist time on the Western Front. (Ransford 1969, pp.134 – 135).

Snakebite
Looking for supplies in a dark barn, a commando called "Swart Lawaai" (Black Blusterer) received a stinging bite. He was carried outside to die, because he had convinced himself that a poisonous snake had bitten him. Whilst one of his comrades read the Bible to the dying man, others went to the barn to see if they could catch the snake. Three men levelled their rifles whilst the fourth investigated a pile of straw with a long pole. Much to the embarrassment of the dying man, they discovered a broody hen, which had defended her five eggs with a sharp peck. Swart Lawaai, after a remarkably short convalescence, recovered his strength, but never his reputation. (Schikkerling, 1964, p.205).

Socialism
A new Colt automatic machine gun was brought to Ladysmith for

evaluation, and it did sterling service during the Battle for Wagon Hill and Caesar's Camp. Macdonald commented: 'One of the men connected with it is said to be a well-known socialist leader, whose projects for levelling the masses have evidently taken a new turn.' (Macdonald, 1999, p.180).

A Royal Field Artillery gun position at Caesar's Camp, Ladysmith.

Sporting chance

During the attack on Red Fort near Bell's Kop, Ladysmith, Robert Reinecke was under severe fire from the British whilst trying to carry a wounded comrade to safety. The Tommies, realizing his predicament, ceased firing, and even allowed him to return to the firing line unmolested. (Reitz, 1929, p.51).

Stampeding cattle

In order to force a way through the line of British posts at Steynskraal, 19 kilometres south of Heidelberg, a party of 150 Boers charged the wire defences behind a herd of stampeding cattle. (Uys, 1981, p.194).

General de Wet and President Steyn escaped from a British trap on 23rd February 1902, near Kalkkrans in the Free State, by rounding up cattle and stampeding them through a guarded pass. "Without mercy, the crazed beasts trampled on those English who could not scatter fast enough. Everybody and everything in their path, including the cannon and machine-guns, were bowled over. Utter confusion reigned. Injured English soldiers tried to crawl away from the flying hooves, whereas others were trampled to death. Those who could escape did so without firing a shot at us". (Uys, 1981, p.215).

State of undress

A commando was trapped by the enemy on the brink of a precipice near Waterval Onder. "In order to escape, they had been obliged to slide down the monkey-ropes and trees, and nearly all their clothing had been torn from their bodies. We met Leipoldt without any trousers, carrying on his back a small Maxim, also many others, more or less naked, and we had many jokes at their expense". (Schikkerling, 1964, p.62).

Staying cool

Deneys Reitz accompanied his uncle on picket duty to a point just 400 yards away from the English defences outside Ladysmith. They drove out on a buckboard, to which they tethered the horses, and then slept on their feather bed, complete with pillows and blankets. (Reitz, 1929, p.62).

During the attack on Wagon Hill, Ladysmith, Reitz was pinned down by British fire in front of Bell's Kop. Bored, he spent the day sleeping and reading a newspaper. His Commando, watching from the rear, thought that he was showing a white flag as he turned the pages of the newspaper, and news spread throughout the laager that his force had surrendered. (Reitz, 1929, p.67).

With Hussar Hill under heavy shelling by the Boers, General Warren had to devise a way of impressing on his troops that they were there to stay. He ordered his batman to warm some water and put it in a small shell hole, and he proceeded to take a bath. General Buller was not impressed when he sent a messenger to Warren requesting him to fetch his orders, and Warren responded by asking the messenger to request Buller in turn to deliver the orders himself. Buller arrived with his large staff on horseback, and Warren got out of his bath and covered himself with a towel. 'General Buller gave me his instructions and then rode off, and I felt I had done what I could for the day to amuse the men—for there was a great crowd of men peeping on, at a respectful distance, and the incident got into the English and Continental papers!' (Coetzer, 1996, p.225 – 226).

Storming a blockhouse

The Boers developed an effective tactic to force the surrender of blockhouses. Some men would direct a heavy fire on the loopholes at a distance from the fort, making it impossible for the defenders to fire. The rest of the men then rushed up to the walls, the covering fire stopped, and the commandos were able to stand

The blockhouse in Krugersdorp, called "Fort Harlech". Note the addition of two bastions on the diagonal.

and shoot through the loopholes. (Kestell, 1976, p.147). With the bullets ricocheting about to devastating effect, the defenders would soon surrender. The British learnt to defend the approaches to the blockhouses with wire entanglements, although the Boers sometimes managed to crawl under the barbed wire and gain the walls. (Schikkerling, 1964, p.236).

The double storey masonry blockhouse, which still stands in Krugersdorp, was originally a square structure. When it was found that the Boers actually had the audacity to attack blockhouses, two bastions were added on the diagonal so that the defenders could enfilade the enemy in case they gained the walls.

Straight-shooting

On a visit under a flag of truce to Commandant David Schoeman's camp in the Steenkampsberg, a British Officer, Alexander, asked the Boers what had become of all their good shots. "Their reply was that they often asked themselves the same question without arriving at a satisfactory conclusion, admitting readily that they were not the marksmen of 20 years ago, though there were still some crack shots among them. Game was not so plentiful as formerly; also many of the population, owing to the mining industry, had been absorbed, so had not handled a rifle for years. With sly humour they pointed out that the English soldiers no longer fought in a red coat and white helmet; in khaki he presented a very inconspicuous target". (Bryant, 1972, p.202).

Many of the major set-piece battles of the war had taken place by mid-December 1899 (Talana, Elandslaagte, Rietfontein, Nicholson's Nek, Belmont, Graspan, Modder River, Stormberg, Magersfontein, and Colenso) before the British discovered that their new Lee Enfield rifles were shooting 18 inches to the right at 500 yards. No wonder that the unfortunate soldiers couldn't shoot straight! This was discovered by recruits of the Imperial Yeomanry during musketry practice, and was due to a problem with the rifles' sighting. 25,000 rifles had to be re-sighted. (Coetzer, 1996, p.24).

General Warren observed that the Boers, being used to the outdoors, had better long-range vision than his troops. "As our men have no knowledge of distances beyond the barrack square, the cricket field or the end of the street, I prefer situations where our moderate-ranged vision can be of more service, such as those of mountain warfare and bush fighting". Many of the British commanders testified at the Commission of Inquiry after the war that distances were often misread because of the clear and clean air, which affected the range of bullets and artillery shells. (Coetzer, 1996, p.114 to 115).

Problems with gun-sights were not confined to the army; the navy also had its problems. Captain Percy Scott of *HMS Terrible* found that the sights of his 9.2-inch guns were wrongly constructed and unserviceable. His 12-pounder guns were mounted so that the gunners were unable to see their targets at all; furthermore the guns could not be loaded as there was not enough room to open the breech. (Coetzer, 1996, p.27).

Mounted Infantry at the head of a British column.

Strategic withdrawal

During the guerrilla phase of the war, the Boers wisely gave way when the ground was unsuitable. On 26th December 1900, while resting after the Battle of Nooitgedacht, a British column approached the Boers from the direction of Potchefstroom. "… as there was no object in fighting except on ground of our own choosing, General Beyers gave them the satisfaction of thinking that we were running away, and at dark we drew off to spend the night near the village of Ventersdorp". (Reitz, 1929, p.143).

T

Tactical changes

By early 1901, the British learnt to emulate some of the Boer fighting tactics and started making night raids. The Boers responded by camping before nightfall, and then, under cover of darkness, moved their camp some distance away. (Schikkerling, 1964, pp.207, 340).

The Boers must have learned this tactic after an unusual night attack on 20th October 1900, when De Wet's famous Commando was thoroughly beaten. After a lot of rain a strong wind arose, and the Commando prepared themselves for a wet night beside the dam on Mr Singleton's farm. Suddenly thousands of frogs emerged from the dam and leaped into the camp, probably as a result of the water being stirred up by the wind. "Here one tumbled on the blanket of a sleeper, then another placed his wet feet on the face of another, and you heard screams in the darkness, as of persons shrinking back from cold baths. It was thought that the attack could be repulsed by blows from hats and boots. But the amphibious enemy had not the least inclination to sound the retreat. They unceasingly renewed the attack, and were continually being supported by fresh reinforcements from the dam. The human beings retreated. Here one man snatched up his bedding and fled—and there another. I must record it. Our warriors lost the battle, and were forced to evacuate their positions before an attack of—frogs!!" (Kestell, 1976, p.135).

Tainted reputation

General Hector Macdonald was wounded and taken prisoner during the first Boer War at the Battle of Majuba, after his heroic defence of "Macdonald's Koppie", having ended up fighting with his bare fists. (Ransford, 1967, p.113). His courage at Majuba so impressed the Boers that Commandant-General Joubert personally handed back his captured sword, saying 'A brave man and his sword should not be separated.' (Ransford, 1967, p.114). Although he had a distinguished career during the Second Anglo Boer War, being affectionately known as "Fighting Mac", he ended up shooting himself in the Hotel Regina in Paris. He had fallen victim to a love affair with a Ceylonese boy, and died like a gentleman to save the reputation of the army and his wife. (Pakenham, 1997, p.574). This was a few days after an audience with King Edward "… who was rumoured to have suggested that only suicide would avert the public scandal of a court-martial". (Ransford, 1967, p.139). MacDonald was one of the few General Officers to have been promoted from the ranks, as a result of his brilliant service in India with Lord Roberts from Kabul to Kandahar. (Hall 2, 1999, p.101).

Tears
At the end of the war the Boer leaders and representatives debated whether to accept the British peace terms. General Wynand Viljoen of the Lydenburg district reported back to the burghers in the field on progress: "He saw stern and rugged men rise to speak. Yet, before they could utter many words, they were choked with emotion and had to wipe away their tears". (Schikkerling, 1964, pp.388 – 389).

The generals
Fighting-General Oosthuizen of the Krugersdorp Commando fought at Majuba, took part in the surrender of Jameson at Doornkop, and distinguished himself during the second Anglo Boer War until he died of wounds received at the Battle of Dwarsvlei. As a Veld-kornet in Natal he captured Winston Churchill after the train was ambushed at Chieveley. (Coetzer, 1976, p.71).

Fighting-General Oosthuizen's grave in Krugersdorp cemetery.

In 1904 Lord Roberts was made redundant by the British Cabinet, He died at the age of 82, as a result of a chill he caught at Bailleul in France. This was at the beginning of the First World War, while he was making his way to the Front to encourage his beloved Indian troops. (Bateman, 1977, p.109). It is with some irony that one of Long's guns (which his only son had died trying to save) was used as a gun carriage at his funeral in 1914. (Coetzer, 1996, p.95).

General Louis Botha was reported to have committed suicide by slitting his wrists on 27th August 1919. This fact was suppressed at the time because he had committed a deed that would not qualify him for a state funeral. At the time he was grossly overweight, depressed, and was recovering from a bout of Spanish flu. (Snyman, 1999, p.127; Pretorius, 1996. p.66). The Botha family and Professor Barnard vehemently deny these claims today. As in the case of General Joubert's execution we shall probably never know the truth.

Captain Congreve, who won a Victoria Cross at Colenso trying to save Long's guns, became a Lieutenant General during the First World War and commanded the XIII Corps at the Battle of the Somme. It was he who ordered the South Africans to "...hold Delville Wood at any cost". (Hall 1, 1999, p.105 – 106). I mention this because the Anglo Boer War had many unforeseen consequences. Who would have thought that a few years after this war, Boer and Brit would be fighting side by side for the Empire? W. A. Beattie's poem about the Battle of Delville Wood expresses this sentiment:

> *Of Boer and British stock were they, and lean and lithe and tanned,*
> *Yet mingling there as brothers fighting for one Motherland;*
> *For kith and kindred o'er the sea, for King and Country now*
> *Their hands they join in fellowship, and took the filial vow.*

On the subject of Delville Wood, it is interesting to note that a memorial cross in Pietermaritzburg, made in 1918 of timber salvaged from the splintered trees of Delville Wood, "weeps" resin on the anniversary of the battle, 14th July, and continues for a week or two. (Uys, 1983, pp.240 – 242). "On 14th July, 121 officers and 3052 other ranks comprised the 1st South African Infantry Brigade. Six days later Colonel Edward Thackeray marched out with two wounded officers and 140 other ranks. Of the survivors one officer and 59 men of the light trench mortar battery had joined as reinforcements two days earlier". (Uys, 1983, p.x).

During the Battle of Rietfontein General Lukas Meyer, one of the Boer patriarchs, suffered a nervous breakdown. This opened the door for young Veld-kornet Louis Botha, who went on to make a name for himself at the battles of Colenso, Spion Kop, Vaalkrans and others, eventually becoming Commandant General of the Transvaal. (Griffith, 1974, p.78).

General French and Major Douglas Haig escaped on the last train out of Ladysmith and were forced to hide under the seats, like ticket dodgers, when their train came under Boer rifle fire. Major Douglas Haig later commanded the British Army in France during the First World War. (Griffith, 1974, p.95).

Lord Methuen and Lord Loch rode ahead of their infantry to a place called Bloedzuikerspan where there was a well served by a Bakkies pump. When the infantry arrived they found the General and Lord Loch operating the pump for the benefit of the parched and travel-worn soldiers. (Guest, 1902, p.10).

After the war General Colvile, sacked by Roberts, was knocked down and killed by a car whilst cycling near Bagshot. Ironically the car was driven by Colonel Rawlinson, who had served on Lord Roberts's staff in South Africa. (Pakenham, 1997, p.574).

General Smith-Dorrien also died as a result of a car accident at Chippenham, Wiltshire. During the Zulu War, serving with the

95th Regiment, he was the only man who escaped from the Battle of Isandlwana on foot. (Hall 2, 1999, p.103). After his distinguished service during the Anglo-Boer War, he commanded the 2nd Army during 1914 – 1915 in France. During the retreat from Mons he saved the British Expeditionary force in defiance of orders from General French by making a stand at Le Cateau. In the deadly silence of a small room in the village of Bertry he said to Generals Allenby and Hamilton: 'Very well, gentlemen, we will fight…' At the time French told him that he was risking a second Sudan. Smith-Dorrien later replied to French, saying, 'I have more to fear from the rear than from the front.' French never sent a reply, but relieved Smith-Dorrien of his command and recalled him to England in April 1915. (Smith-Dorrien, 1925, p.401).

The legend of the flowers
In the Ventersdorp cemetery a British soldier, Private George Shaw, is buried in unconsecrated ground, far away from his comrades. As a result of some remarkable research, Mr J.G. Orford pieced together an unusual and romantic story about this grave. The 1st Loyal North Lancs, Private Shaw's regiment, was engaged in farm burning operations in the Western Transvaal. On one occasion three women were turned out of their farmhouse and, as it was set alight, one of the young women wept bitterly. Shaw was so upset that he remonstrated with his commanding officer about the cruel and destructive farm-burning policy. The exasperated officer said, 'Well Shaw, if you don't like it, why don't you go and fight for the Boers?'

It appears that Shaw did indeed desert and joined the Boers as an unarmed transport rider. He fell in love with a Boer girl (probably the one who instigated his desertion) and spent many happy hours with her, helping her with household chores. He was once captured by the British, but was not recognized, and escaped to rejoin his girlfriend, Martha Engelbrecht. When he was captured a second time his military training gave him away: he stood to attention when rations were issued to him. He was immediately court-martialled and sentenced to be shot. Sentence was carried out in a very cruel way. Instead of being shot standing up, he was tied sitting in a chair, and the firing squad deliberately missed with their first volley. Martha watched his cruel execution from the cover of some bushes.

Soon after his execution she planted a pepper tree on the left of the grave and a pine tree on the right. She eventually married a friend of Shaw's called Fleischer. Every Friday morning, before the cemetery opened, she placed flowers on Shaw's grave. Her weekly pilgrimage continued for over 50 years until she became too old to visit the cemetery. On her final visit she left some caskets of everlasting flowers on the grave. At her funeral few people knew what the minister meant when he quoted from the Old Testament, Song of Songs: "Many waters cannot quench the fires of love, neither can the floods drown it". (Orford, 1977, pp.61 – 62). Today you can see George Shaw's lonely cast-iron cross in Ventersdorp cemetery, alongside the pine tree which Martha planted so many years ago—sadly the pepper tree was cut down a few years ago to make way for a stormwater drain. Sit in Martha's ancient apple orchard and read *Song of Songs*, chapter 8 verses 6 to 7—the woman's words to her lover:

Private Shaw's cast-iron cross in Ventersdorp cemetery as it was a number of years ago. Note the pepper tree on the left of the grave and the pine tree on the right.

Private Shaw's grave as it is now.

Under the apple tree I woke you,
in the place where you were born.
Close your heart to every love but mine;
hold no one in your arms but me.
Love is as powerful as death;
passion is as strong as death itself.
It bursts into flame and burns like a raging fire.
Water cannot put it out;
no flood can drown it. (Bible, 1976, p.741).

On 17th January 2000 I re-visited Ventersdorp with my partner, Roger Webster, a fellow historian. He introduced me to Martha's son, John Fleisher, and we were able to complete Orford's story. We established that Private Shaw succeeded in preventing the destruction of Martha's house, and we found it near the villiage—a partially ruined "Hartebeeshuis". Nearby is the delightful Victorian home, dating back to 1884, where Martha and John brought up John Fleisher junior. Martha's garden is scattered with very old pepper and pine trees, where she must have obtained the seedlings that she planted beside George's grave. John Fleisher directed us to his mother's grave in Ventersdorp cemetery (nos 128 and 129): Martha Engelbrecht

John and Martha Fleisher's grave in Ventersdorp cemetery.

The Hartebeeshuis where Martha Engelbrecht grew up, and where she met George Shaw during a British farm-burning expedition. This photograph is taken from Martha's apple orchard and shows the ancient pepper tree on the left, and the pine tree on the right.

was born on 1ˢᵗ October 1877 and died on 18ᵗʰ September 1957, seven years after John Fleisher.

Theft

General Ben Viljoen had occasion to reprimand some commandos who had taken absence without leave. While he was reprimanding them, one of his two shirts, which he had hung out to dry, was stolen. (Schikkerling, 1964, p.200).

Being short of fuel, on 11ᵗʰ February 1901, the Boers uprooted all the wooden telegraph poles between Belfast and Dullstroom. (Schikkerling, 1964, p.146).

As the Boers were preparing to leave Hectorspruit to escape the victorious British Army, through what is today the Kruger National Park, they became adept at stealing from one another. "Cattle, wagons, saddles, harness and boxes of tinned dainties, were stolen and re-stolen back and forth, countless times a day. Meeting Manie Mentz, I obtained from him for our journey, one case of cocoa, one of jam, and one of condensed milk. Then, while I went round the corner for further supplies, these were irrecoverably stolen". (Schikkerling, 1964, p.66).

Too many chiefs

Confusion reigned as to which British officer was in charge on the summit of Spion Kop. General Warren, at the suggestion of General Buller, had appointed Colonel Thorneycroft in command after General Woodgate was mortally wounded, but neglected to tell anyone except Thorneycroft. General Coke arrived later on the summit with reinforcements, thinking that he was now in command. When the Scottish Rifles under Colonel Cook arrived, being senior to Colonel Thorneycroft, he thought he was in command, and had an argument with Thorneycroft before going to General Coke for adjudication. Coke added to the confusion by declaring that he was in overall command but that another new arrival, Colonel Hill of the Middlesex Regiment, was the senior soldier on the summit. (Griffith, 1974, p.269).

Later General Warren completely forgot about his earlier appointment of Thorneycroft and asked General Coke to give command temporarily to Thorneycroft when he recalled Coke from the summit for consultations. (Griffith, 1974, p.273).

Torture

During an attack on armed Blacks on 17th February 1902, a Boer called Venter went missing. His badly mutilated body was found five days later, having been tortured to death. While he was alive his ears were cut off, and both of his legs chopped off above the knee. He lived until the morning, when he was found by the sweetheart of one of the Blacks killed during the attack. "She sat alongside of the mutilated man and slowly thrust a spear into different parts of his body until he died". (Schikkerling, 1964, p.360).

A Black National Scout called Simon disappeared after a skirmish in the Free State. A notice was found written in pencil on the whitewashed walls of a farmhouse. "Pray to God you're not caught for we will shoot everyone of you as we did Simon and the English officer too who leads you. John Straightman". Simon's body was later found near a place called Doornbult. He had been shot in many places: through the knee, heart, breast, head and elbow. It was clear by signs on the ground that after his capture he had been tied to a horse's tail and dragged for about 400 yards, with Boers shooting at him from a distance. (Fuller, 1937, p.252).

Trafalgar

In the same spirit that Lord Nelson ignored orders at Trafalgar, Colonel Buchanan-Riddell of the 60th Rifles ignored General Lyttelton's lunatic order to abandon Twin Peaks during the Battle of Spion Kop. The capture of Twin Peaks was the only sensible move the British had made during the battle and would have led to their victory. At 6 pm Colonel Buchanan-Riddell was killed and, on being advised by Lyttelton that they would get no support from the thousands of idle soldiers in the camp, Major Bewicke-Copley (his second-in-command.) withdrew his troops. (Griffith, 1974, p.271).

Aloe Knoll and Twin Peaks from the main British trench on Spion Kop. Aloe Knoll is the nearest hill, with Twin Peaks behind it.

Treasure found

A Boer camped at a farmhouse set out a trail of mealies attached to fishhooks to capture some chickens, which he succeeded in doing. Later he found a diamond in one of the chicken's stomachs, which he sold for £9. After the war, he secured the right to prospect in the area and to purchase the farm at a nominal price. He successfully mined the diamonds and became a wealthy man. (Schikkerling, 1964, p.302).

Trenches

Trenches were first used successfully at the Battle of Cerignola in 1503, when the Spanish defeated the French. However, Delarey's use of trenches at Magersfontein caught the British by surprise. In spite of their observation balloons, the British did not detect a 20 kilometre defence line that consisted of carefully camouflaged trenches, stone sangars, and earthworks. (Bateman, 1977, p.79).

Despite the system of blockhouses built along the railway lines, the Boer commandos persisted in crossing at night with their wagons, cattle and horses. In order to prevent their wagons from crossing, the British had to dig hundreds of kilometres of trenches parallel to the railway line. A good example, which has survived the years, can be seen between Wonderfontein and Belfast in Mpumalanga.

A surviving example of the trenches dug parallel to the railway lines to prevent the Boers crossing with their wagons at night.

Tribute

After the war, General Botha realized that the only hope for South Africa lay in a reconciliation of the differences between English and Dutch, and that some grand gesture should be made. Accordingly in August 1907, he proposed to the Transvaal Government that they acquire the recently discovered Cullinan diamond and present it to King Edward. The gift was to be a token of the loyalty of the people of the Transvaal and in commemoration of the grant of Responsible Government. The King was advised to refuse the gift because the Transvaal was "...too poor to make such a kingly gift". He finally accepted it as, "The token of the loyalty and attachment of the people of the Transvaal to my throne and person". When the diamond was cut the largest portion, 516.5 ct, went into the King's crown, and another gem of 309 ct was set aside for the Queen's crown. (Chilvers, 1930, pp.123 – 124).

U

Underwear
The British captured the personal belongings of the Russian-Dutch ambulance, which was assisting the Boers, shortly before Pretoria surrendered. In gentlemanly fashion it was returned to them in St Petersburg some time later. (Izedinova, 1977, p.191).

"Die Berg", the site of Commandant Schoeman's Laager.

Commandant Schoeman had his laager at "Die Berg", a prominent position east of Lydenburg. The Rifle Brigade drove him from his laager after an attack, and a few days later, a cape-cart approached the British camp at Lydenburg under a white flag. When the elderly Boer driver was asked why he had come in a cart and not on a horse, he replied that he had a letter from his commandant for the British general, and that he knew the contents. The British had taken the trunk containing the commandant's underwear when they looted the camp. "Now if your general agrees", Schoeman wrote, "that robbing a man of his spare vests and pants is not playing the game in civilized warfare, the necessary articles may be restored, and I cannot carry a portmanteau on horseback". The general returned his underwear and the old burgher remarked to his escort as he left them, 'You English fight fair!' (Bryant, 1972, p.204).

"A Four in Hand", an example of Victorian pornography.

Unfortunate decision

At nightfall on the day of the Battle of Spion Kop, the British were in a favourable position in spite of the terrible slaughter that had taken place. Artillery was on its way up, as were reinforcements, sandbags, and communications equipment. The Boers had largely abandoned the Kop, and Thorneycroft's men were tired but determined to stick it out. Suddenly rifle fire flared up on the British right flank and this was just enough to break

Thorneycroft's resolve, and he gave orders to abandon Spion Kop. Unbeknown to him the fire came from just a handful of burghers led by Commandant Prinsloo, who was trying to recover his brother's body before abandoning the Kop. Although Thorneycroft was exhausted and sickened by the slaughter, he made three tactical mistakes after nightfall which turned the British victory into a humiliating defeat: he made no attempt to reconnoitre the Boer positions after dark; with 5,000 men at his disposal on the Kop, he made no attempt to probe the Boers with a night attack; when he abandoned the Kop he gave no consideration to leaving a small holding force, and there was no determined attempt to remove all the wounded. (Ransford, 1969, p.101).

Uniforms

By July 1901, Boer uniforms were getting really interesting. "He wore knickerbockers, his bulging calves were enclosed in a pair of lady's stockings, and in his hat he sported a white feather. The assemblage looked very much like a cannibal fancy dress meeting. One officer wore a jacket of monkey skin, hair to the outside; another officer a jacket of leopard skin. One looked a cross between Attila the Hun, and Sancho Panza. Others wore odd garments of sheep, goat, and deerskin, and of green baize and gaudily coloured blankets. Quite evidently the apparel does not here proclaim the man. Only last week, a man who bore the remains of one of his friends to the grave was decked out in green baize trousers and a dress suit jacket". (Schikkerling, 1964, p.250).

"Kokkie addressed the court, emphasizing with his right-hand, while with his left he held up his trousers, and in some fashion kept together also his coat which was split open the whole length of his back". (Schikkerling, 1964, p.253).

During the final (successful) attempt to relieve Ladysmith a Prussian officer, Colonel von Braun, was taken prisoner. The Tommies were fascinated by the fact that he wore an oilskin coat reinforced with steel netting. (Griffith, 1974, p.328).

In September 1901, Schikkerling's Commando passed through a village in the north-eastern Transvaal, and was greeted enthusiastically by the local women and children. "We who were gaily dressed rode up to them and accepted flowers and milk; others who had no trousers, or were clothed in grain bags and bits of blanket or carpet, kilt-fashion, rode on the far side. Fortunately I was able to put my best foot forward, and the boot showing my sunburned toes remained on the starboard side. I was dressed for a left-hand view". (Schikkerling, 1964, p.305).

Unwanted gratitude

After the successful night attack by General Muller on Monument Hill (also known as Fosberry's Post) near Belfast, piercing cries

The Monument at Fosberry's Post (Monument Hill) near Belfast. Note the bullet marks resulting from General Muller's night attack.

for help were heard from a deep and open latrine. "Someone risked going forward, and by holding down his gun, with much difficulty, rescued the half-drowned man, who said his leg had been shot off. The soldier in his misery kept hopping after his saviour, who, holding his nostrils, shouted 'Don't come so close!'" (Schikkerling, 1964, p.129).

Manned by 83 men of the 1st The Royal Irish Regiment under Captain Fosberry, the garrison was overwhelmed after a desperate fight in which Fosberry was one of the 40 men killed or wounded. Private J. Barry was posthumously awarded the Victoria Cross for gallantry in rendering the post's Maxim gun useless. (Jones, 1999, p.153).

Useless booty

The morning after the Heidelbergers' looting of the wrecked goods train near Greylingstad, they opened a large chest labelled "Handle with Care". There was much amusement when they found that it contained wax dolls and dolls' prams. (Uys, 1981, p.115).

With soldiers hot on their heels, two burghers raided some Indian stores near Vereeniging and quickly grabbed anything they could. When they reached their camp they were disappointed to find that much of the booty consisted of women's underwear and baby clothes. (Uys, 1981, p.141).

V

Vegetables

Veld-kornet van As and his Commando ambushed two carts and a mule cart laden with fresh vegetables, destined for the National Scouts in Heidelberg. The three drivers, two of whom they knew well from pre-war days, were made to strip. The Boers then placed pumpkins on their heads and made them walk back to Heidelberg. (Uys, 1981, p.220).

Mealies were the most important source of food for the Boer commandos. "It is our meat and drink and all that sustains our animals. It is eaten green and ripe, boiled and roasted, in porridge and in cakes. It is also toasted and treated as 'coffee'. Take it away and we could not remain in the field ten days longer. Without it we would have had to abandon the war more than a year ago. A mealie cob should be on our coat of arms, to which it has more claim that all the fond images thereon". (Schikkerling, 1964, p.326). Schikkerling's wish was granted nearly 100 years later when a mealie cob was incorporated into the coat of arms of North West Province.

W

War graves

During the war British soldiers were buried close to where they fell, which has proved to be of great value to military historians searching for skirmish and battle sites. However, this has been an obstacle to farmers, dam and road-builders, and urban developers. In the 1960s the War Graves Commission supervised the exhumation and relocation of scattered graves and small cemeteries into the bigger towns. In Krugersdorp, for example, there is a memorial to the hundreds of soldiers who have been re-buried there, and the lists of names by Regiment (and sometimes date of death) do not have any additional details and hardly attract notice. However, there are often interesting stories attached to these names. The second name listed under

Consolidated war grave in Krugersdorp cemetery, including Lt Borghuys, Kitchener's Horse.

"Kitchener's Horse" on the memorial in Krugersdorp cemetery is that of Lieutenant Borghys (spelt elsewhere as Borghuys). On Thursday 29th November 1900, Sergeant-Major Carpenter demanded a weekend pass from his lieutenant. When this was refused he shot Lieutenant Borghys. Needless to say, Carpenter was court-martialled and executed on 18th December 1900. Carpenter's grave is unrecorded, but is probably located outside of consecrated ground, as was the practice at the time.

Lists of new graves were made by the Guild of Loyal Women (which later became the Victoria League, and then became defunct). Cast-iron crosses in various designs were procured from different factories in Cape Town, and the Guild was subsidized to the tune of half-a-crown per cross by the Government. The Women's spelling and writing were not the best, hence a lot of discrepancies between the information on the crosses and the burial records. Only one name register has survived—the other registers must be in safekeeping somewhere, but they have never been found.

The grave of Nurse Gluyas in Maraisburg cemetery, Roodepoort.

Close to the grave of Captain Meyrick in the Maraisburg cemetery, Roodepoort, is a cast-iron cross dated 12th January 1906, to the memory of Nurse Lydia Gluyas who died at the age of 48. In 1989, as I commenced research on this grave with the National Monuments Council, a great-nephew of Lydia wrote to the Council from New Zealand to inquire about her last resting-place. Mr Carruthers, her great-nephew, wrote to say that Lydia had been a nurse at various hospitals around London and had joined up as an army nurse during the war, when there was a call for "Young ladies of good character and address" to go to South Africa. She put her age back by six years, and was accepted for service. She fell in love with South Africa and after the war decided to live here, but only enjoyed peace for four years. According to Mr Carruthers, "She was quite an accomplished artist and used to send my mother several paintings and drawings she made around South Africa. Sadly few if any have survived over the years, and I think it may be owing to a poor war-time grade of paper which just crumbled away to powder".

On the subject of the exhumation and relocation of war graves to make way for "progress", a South African archaeologist, Elizabeth Voight of the Transvaal Museum, commented in her 1984 report entitled *Report on Military Burials on the farm Elandspruit, district Lydenburg*: "... I believe that more honour would have been given to the dead if the gravestones alone had been moved and a simple monument erected above the future water level of the dam, indicating that the original place of rest lay beneath the waters". Her account of the exhumation of the Strathcona's Horse mass grave is interesting. "The length of the grave and the extended position of the leg bones suggest that the men may have been buried in a sitting position with their legs extended straight in front of them". We sometimes find mass graves, which are aligned north-south instead of east-west (e.g. Chieveley), and this would be a logical explanation. Also of interest from this report (and for the information of would-be grave robbers) very few artefacts remain in anything like recognizable condition, owing to the generally acidic nature of the soil in South Africa.

General Andy Wauchope, killed at Magersfontein, was buried at Matjiesfontein, hundreds of kilometres away. This is reputed to be as a result of a misunderstanding. (Bateman, 1977, p.23).

Baden-Powell's simple grave in Nyeri, Kenya, has only his last name on it and the Boy Scout trail sign for "I have gone home"—a dot within a circle. (Bateman, 1977, p.89).

Water
Some springs were found halfway up Spion Kop, which gave the troops some relief. (Coetzer, 1996, p.147). During their retreat the troops slaked their thirst there, until they were told that the medics had been using the water to wash out wounds. (Griffith, 1974, p.275).

The site of the British dressing station during the Battle of Spion Kop, looking towards the ascent route. The spring is half-way down the steep slope to the left of the dressing station.

A man was having a relaxing bath on his verandah in Ladysmith when a shell bounced off a tree and hit the house without exploding. It then rolled along the verandah and upset the bathtub and its lucky occupant. (Macdonald, 1999, p.73).

Towards the end of the Siege of Ladysmith a German engineer arrived to supervise the construction of a dam on the Klip River, which would be used to flood the town. On Sunday 25th February 1900 the Anglican vicar appropriately preached a sermon on Noah and the great flood. (Griffith, 1974, p.296). The Boer attempt was unsuccessful.

The site of the Boer dam, built in an attempt to flood besieged Ladysmith. This is on the Klip River near Intombi Camp.

With the Highveld winter setting in, the colonel of the 1st Rifle Brigade issued orders forbidding any man to wash himself before 11.00 am. 'He does not like cold water himself!' was Private Tucker's comment. On 6th June 1900, nine men were caught bathing a few minutes before 11.00 am and sentenced to eight days defaulters. "Another typical indication of the sort of man we have in charge of us". (Tucker, 1980, pp.109 – 110).

What if?
What if Winston Churchill had been wounded at the Battle of Spion Kop? Mahatma Ghandi, who was a stretcher-bearer there, might have taken him to the field hospital. Instead, they became

bitter adversaries in later life, with Churchill referring to him as "That half-naked Fakir". (Griffith, 1974, p.272).

White flag

Captain R.C.H. Miers of the South African Constabulary, based in Heidelberg, used to visit the Boer commandos under a white flag to try to persuade them to give up the struggle. On 25th September 1901, he approached Veld-kornet van As and two burghers in their observation post. Van As sent one of the burghers, Louis Slabbert, to meet him to ensure that he did not get close to the observation post. After refusing to stop, Miers, who was armed with a revolver, rode up to Van As and Du Toit. A shot was fired and Miers fell off his horse, dead, his revolver rolling away. Van As claimed that Miers drew his revolver and aimed at him before he shot him. After the war, in spite of General Louis Botha's assurances that he would not be harmed, Van As was tried by the British and sentenced to death. On 23rd June 1902, Van As was executed by a ten-man firing squad of the Somersets at the back of the old jail at Heidelberg. His

Lt Miers's grave in Kloof cemetery, Heidelberg.

body was dumped into a pan 600 metres away, but he was later re-buried in the Kloof cemetery (near Miers). The British government later admitted to Van As's father that he had not been given a fair trial, and that the conviction and sentence were unjust. (Uys, 1981, pp.172 – 175; 231 – 232).

The spot where Veld-kornet van As was executed, behind the Heidelberg jail. The bullet marks are visible in the granite block just above my son's head.

Wild animals

During the engagement between the Liverpool Regiment and the Heidelberg Commando at Geluk (leading up to the Battle of Bergendal), a steenbok burst through the British lines towards the Boers. Both sides fired at it and at times it was completely covered in dust from the near misses. However, it disappeared into the ridges unscathed, and the soldiers resumed their fight. (Uys, 1981, p.66).

Near Fourteen Streams a lyddite shell exploded at the entrance to a jackal's lair. He bounded out of another entrance and ran off, tail between his legs. (Izedinova, 1977, p.160).

In 1962 gunner Archie Wilson recalled an incident in the Eastern Transvaal. "There was no Reserve (now the Kruger National Park) when I was in S.A.; in fact we had an outpost killed by lions one night. That happened in the Bushvelde away near Amsterdam in the very far Eastern Transvaal".

When camped near Moordenaar's Poort in the northern Cape, and hard-pressed by the British, Smuts's Commando was rendered helpless for a number of hours by a porcupine. It had wandered through the camp at night and stampeded the horses. (Reitz, 1929, p.211).

At the height of the Battle of Three Tree Hill on 20th January 1900, a hare dashed through the British infantry. About 100 of them leapt up from their firing positions and chased the hare, regardless of danger, but it got away safely. (Griffith, 1974, p.256).

General de Wet, when challenged by General Joubert on his decision to give the burghers two weeks' leave after the fall of Bloemfontein, responded: 'I cannot catch a hare, General, with unwilling dogs.' (Trew, 1999, p.182).

SOURCES

Baker, D.C. (Dec 1998) *Military History Journal*: vol 11 no 2. Johannesburg: South African National Museum of Military History. (Baker).

Bateman, Philip (1977) *Generals of the Anglo-Boer War*. Cape Town: Purnell and Sons (Pty) Ltd. (Bateman).

Bosman, Herman Charles (1964) *Mafeking Road*. Cape Town: Central News Agency Ltd. (Bosman).

Bryant, Arthur (1972) *Jackets of Green*. London: William Collins Sons & Co Ltd. (Bryant).

Cassell's history of the Boer War 1899 – 1902 (1903). London: Cassell and Company Ltd. (Cassell).

Chilvers, Hedley H. (1930) *The Seven Lost Trials of Africa*. London: Cassell and Company Ltd. (Chilvers).

Coetzer, O. (1996) *Road to Infamy*. Johannesburg: Waterman Publications. (Coetzer).

Creswicke, Louis (circa 1902) *South Africa and the Transvaal War*. Edinburgh: The Caxton Publishing Co. (Creswicke).

Crow, Bella (Unpublished diary). Ladysmith Museum. (Bella Crow).

Crow, George (1903) *The Commission of HMS Terrible 1898 – 1902*. George Newness Ltd. (Crow).

Crum, Maj F.M. (1903) *With the Mounted Infantry in South Africa being side-lights on the Boer Campaign 1899 – 1902*. Cambridge: MacMillan and Bowes. (Crum).

De Klerk, Dr Willem (Editor in Chief) (1987) *Krugersdorp 100 Years*. Krugersdorp: Town Council of Krugersdorp. (De Klerk).

De Wet, C.R. (1902) *Three Years' War*. Westminster: Archibald Constable and Co. Ltd. (De Wet).

Dictionary of South African biography vol 2 (1972). Pretoria: Human Sciences Research Council. (DSAB).

Eliot, T.S. (Ed.) (1963) *A Choice of Kipling's Verse*. London: Faber and Faber Limited. (Eliot).

Fuller, Maj-Gen J.F.C. (1937) *The Last of the Gentleman's Wars—a subaltern's journal of the War in SA*. London: Faber and Faber Ltd. (Fuller).

Good News Bible. (1976) Bible Society of South Africa. (Bible).

Grabandt, Kees (Compiler) (1985) *Weeds of Crops and Gardens in Southern Africa*. Johannesburg: Ciba-Geigy (Pty) Ltd. (Grabandt).

Great Britain: Parliament Command Paper Cd. 893 (1902). (C. Paper).

Griffith, Kenneth (1974) *Thank God we kept the Flag Flying*. London: Hutchinson & Co. (Griffith).

Guest, H.M. (1902) *With Lord Metheun and the 1st Division*. Klerksdorp: H.M. Guest. (Guest).

Hall, D. (1999) *Halt! Action Front! with Colonel Long at Colenso*. Weltevreden Park: Covos-Day Books. (Hall 1).

Hall, D. (1999) *The Hall Handbook of the Anglo-Boer War 1899 – 1902*. Scottsville: The University of Natal Press. (Hall 2).

Hamilton, I.B.M (1966) *The Happy Warrior, a life of General Sir Ian Hamilton GCB, GCMG, DSO*. London: Cassell and Company Ltd. (Hamilton).

Harfield, Maj A.G. (1981) *Early Signalling Equipment: Pamphlet no 1 "The Heliograph"*. Royal Signals Museum, Blandford Camp. (Harfield).

Izedinova, Sophia (1977) *A few months with the Boers*. Johannesburg: Perskor Publishers. (Izediniova).

Jones, H.M. & M.G.M. (1999) *A Gazetteer of the Second Anglo-Boer War 1899 – 1902*. London: The Military Press. (Jones).

Kaplan, Mendel & Roberts, Marian (Editors) (1991) *Founders and Followers—Johannesburg Jewry 1887 – 1915*. Cape Town: Vlaeberg Publishers cc. (Kaplan).

Keliher, J.J. & Co Ltd (1904) *The official records of the Guards Brigade in South Africa*. London: (ORGB).

Kestell, J.D. (1976) *Through Shot and Flame*. Johannesburg: Africana Book Society (Pty) Ltd. (Kestell).

Lee, Emanoel (1985) *To the Bitter End*. New York: Viking Penguin Inc. (Lee).

Lowry, Rev E.P. (1902) *With the Guards Brigade from Bloemfontein to Koomati Poort and Back*. London: Horace Marshall & Son. (Lowry).

Macdonald, D. (1999) *How we kept the Flag Flying*. Weltevredenpark: Covos-Day Books. (Macdonald).

Maurice, Maj-Gen Sir Frederick & Grant, Capt M.H. (1906 – 1910) *History of the War in South Africa, 1899 - 1902*. London: Hurst and Blackett Ltd. (Maurice).

McFadden, P. (1999) *The Battle of Elandslaagte*. Randburg: Ravan Press. (McFadden).

Muller, C.H. (1936) *Oorlogsherinneringe*. Cape Town: Nasionale Pers. (Muller).

Orford, J.G. (December 1971) *Military History Journal*: vol 2 no 2. Johannesburg. (Orford).

Orford, J.G. (December 1977) *Military History Journal*: vol 4 no 2. Johannesburg. (Orford).

Pakenham, Thomas (1997) *The Boer War*. Johannesburg: Jonathan Ball Publishers (Pty) Ltd. (Pakenham).

Pretorius, P.J. (1996) *Volksverraad*. Mossel Bay: Libanon Uitgewers. (Pretorius).

Ransford, Oliver (1967) *The Battle of Majuba Hill—the First Boer War*. London: John Murray.

Ransford, Oliver (1969) *The Battle of Spion Kop*. London: The Camelot Press Ltd.

Reitz, Deneys (1929) *Commando—a Boer journal of the Boer War*. London: Faber and Faber Ltd. (Reitz).

Romer, Maj C.F. and Mainwaring Maj A.E. (1908) *The Second Battalion Royal Dublin Fusiliers in the South African War*. London: A. L. Humphreys. (Romer).

Rosenthal, E. (1975) *The Best of Eric Rosenthal.* Cape Town: Howard Timmins.

Schikkerling, R. W. (1964) *Commando Courageous.* Hugh Keartland (Publishers) (Pty) Ltd. (Schikkerling).

Schoeman, J. (1950) *Generaal Hendrik Schoeman—was hy 'n veraaier?* Broederstroom (Pretoria): J.Schoeman. (Schoeman).

Scholtz, G.D. (1940) *In Doodsgevaar: Die Oorlogservarings van Kapt J.J. Naude.* Johannesburg: Voortrekker Pers. (Scholtz).

Smith-Dorrien, Gen Sir Horace (1925) *Memories of Forty-Eight years' service.* London: John Murray. (Smith-Dorrien).

Snyman, Adriaan (1999) *Voice of a Prophet.* Mossel Bay: Vaandel Publishers. (Snyman).

Todd, P. and Fordham, D. (Compilers) (1980) *Private Tucker's Boer War diary.* London: Elm Tree Books.

Trew, P. (1999) *The Boer War Generals.* Jeppestown: Jonathan Ball Publishers (Pty) Ltd. (Trew).

Uys, Ian (1981) *Heidelbergers of the Boer War.* Johannesburg: Uys Publishers. (Uys).

Uys, Ian (1983) *Delville Wood.* Johannesburg: Uys Publishers. (Uys).

Viljoen, B. (1903). *My Reminiscences of the Anglo-Boer War.* London: Hood, Douglas & Howard. (Viljoen).

INDEX

WELCOME TO COVOS-DAY BOOKS

Southern Africa's newest publishing house

ate 1997, in Johannesburg, Covos-Day Books began life as a part-time, "mailorder-from-
ne" business – with one title. We soon appreciated that the southern African market was not
ig adequately serviced in terms of non-fiction – military, historical and socio-political
terial. In a short space of time, we have established ourselves as a leading African publisher in
se fields. This year, 2000, we publish 14 new titles. We are now expanding into international
rkets and our books are being enthusiastically received.

late, our focus has been the Anglo-Boer War and the southern African "bush wars" of the
0s and 1980s. However, this year we shall also be developing other categories, including
thern African fiction, literature and auto/biography. Without losing sight of our core
iness, we are, however, not afraid to explore other diverse and exciting areas – from war
try – to accounts of Japanese POWs in World War II – and ANC exiles during the Apartheid era.

publishing business in Africa is alive and well – producing top quality books that are vibrant,
rtaining and historically relevant. Keep an eye out for our titles!

---

es indicated in this catalogue are recommended retail prices in South Africa, United Kingdom, USA, Canada,
ralia and New Zealand.

's may vary slightly and are subject to change without notice.

 specifications and publication dates are, in some instances, provisional.

VOS-DAY BOOKS

 Box 6996
tevredenpark, 1715
th Africa

+2711-475 0922
+2711-475 8974
il: covos@global.co.za
site at **www.mazoe.com**

ign by **JANT Design**, Centurion, South Africa.
il: j.design@mweb.co.za

NEW TITLES

BELOVED AFRICAN
Jill Baker

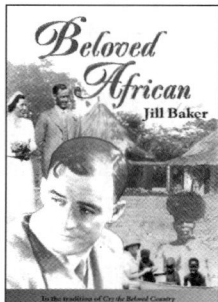

The author, among Zimbabwe's, previously Rhodesia's, best-loved media personalities, writes about her enigmatic father, John Hammond, one of that country's earliest and foremost educators. A pioneer at the turn of the century, he helped forge the solid educational system that spawned some of the great minds of the country, including many of the founding black nationalists. A controversial, but much-loved figure.

In the same vein as "Cry the Beloved Country"

Hardback; 228 x 155mm; 508 pages; 58 b/w photographs, map; 0 620 24117 9

R165.00	£20.00	US$30.00	C$40.00	A$40.00	NZ$55.00

VLAMGAT – The Story of the Mirage F1 in the South African Air Force
Brigadier Dick Lord

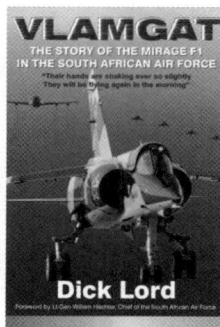

The sequel to *Fire, Flood and Ice,* this is an outstanding compilation of stories and experiences of SAAF Mirage pilots who operated in the Angolan and the SWA/Namibian bush wars. The author, an ex-Top Gun and Fleet Air Arm pilot, was one time the CO of 1 Squadron (Mirages), the SAAF. A thrilling account told "from cockpit".

Hardback; 228 x 155mm; 380 pages; 55 colour, 169 b/w photographs, maps, diagrams; 0 620 24116 0

R185.00	£20.00	US$35.00	C$45.00	A$45.00	NZ$60.

BOMBARDMENT OF LADYSMITH ANTICIPATED
– The Diary of a Siege
Alan Chalmers

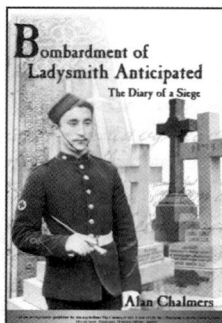

Into the cauldron of the siege of Ladysmith arrived the slight, Chaplinesque figure George Maidment, a British Army orderly, fresh out from the Midlands of England For over 100 days he recorded the events of the siege in his diary – the daily tediu the fighting, the sniping, the lack of food, the disgust at eating their own horses. O bungled relief attempt after another as the great British Army was put through its paces by a bunch of farmers. This is a story of great courage lying alongside great stupidity, of world events alongside the personal, intimate observations of a local h

"Of the myriad books published for the Anglo-Boer War Centenary thi is one of the best illustrated and most well written" *– Meurig Jones, Chairman, Victorian Military Society*

Softback; 222 x 152mm; 340 pages; 298 b/w illustrations; 9 foldout maps; 0 620 24996 X

R140.00	£15.00	US$25.00	C$35.00	A$35.00	NZ$45

NEW TITLES

E FEAR NAUGHT BUT GOD

ul Els

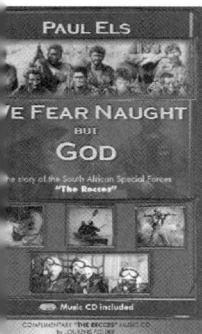

The story of the South African Special Forces ("The Recces"), from inception in the 1960s to disbandment in 1993. A unique account of one of South Africa's premier units, masters in the art of reconnaissance and clandestine warfare. Pro rata, the most highly decorated unit during the wars in Angola and Namibia/SWA.

Includes a free copy of Lourens Fourie's music CD "The Recces"

Softback; 222 x 152mm; approx. 320 pages; approx. 200 b/w illustrations, maps
0 620 23891 7

R140.00	£15.00	US$25.00	C$35.00	A$35.00	NZ$45.00

RE IN THE SKY – The Destruction of the Orange Free State 1899-1902

en Coetzer

A shocking account of Britain's official Boer War policy of scorched earth, farm burning and concentration camps. "More than 27,000 people", mainly women and children, died in appalling conditions. It was a mistake, Milner later wrote. But a brutal one, the consequences of which are still felt today. An in-depth, horrifying exposé.

Softback; 222 x 152mm; 383 pages; 49 b/w photographs, map; 0 620 24114 4

R120.00	£15.00	US$25.00	C$35.00	A$35.00	NZ$45.00

AFEKING!

lcolm Flower-Smith and Edmund Yorke

Psychologically affected by the fact that it was from Mafeking that the Jameson Raid was launched, the Boers determined to regain this key town. The exceptional military leadership, indomitable spirit and personal charisma of Colonel Baden-Powell made him the ideal officer for the British defence – the source of inspiration for the defenders of Mafeking during the epic 7½-month siege. By March 1900, the garrison was famished; death and destruction had become daily fare. When, in May, Mafeking was finally relieved, the British nation was swept by a wave of patriotic hysteria, unequalled since.

With the foreword by The Honourable Mrs Betty Clay CBE, daughter of Lord Baden-Powell

Softback; 222 x 150mm; approx. 185 pages; approx. 48 b/w illustrations; 0 620 25251 0

R100.00	£10.00	US$17.50	C$25.00	A$25.00	NZ$32.50

CURRENTLY AVAILABLE

PAMWE CHETE – The Legend of the Selous Scouts
Lieutenant-Colonel Ron Reid-Daly

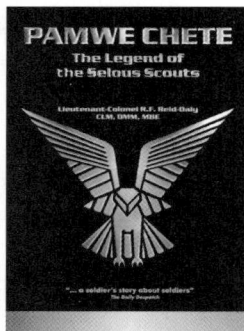

The revamped, rewritten version of the best-selling *Top Secret War*. With new, previously unpublished material, including the roll of honour and full schedule citations and wings. New photo sections. The definitive account of this exceptior unit's short but distinguished service in the field of pseudo counter-insurgency operations during the bitter Rhodesian bush war. A classic.

Hardback; 228 x 155mm; 664 pages; 150 b/w illustrations, maps; 0 620 237

R225.00	£27.50	US$45.00	C$60.00	A$60.00	NZ$75.0

FIREFORCE – One Man's War in the Rhodesian Light Infantry
Chris Cocks

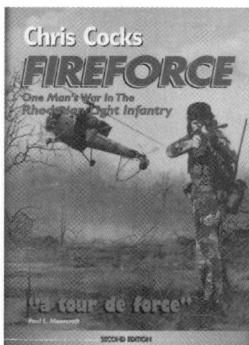

Widely acclaimed as the classic account of counter-insurgency warfare in Africa told by the combat soldier "on the ground". The gut-wrenching account of bru face-to-face combat in the bush, this is not for the squeamish. Has been comp with *Commando* and *Dispatches*. Includes the RLI roll of honour, citations an operational orders, as appendices.

"A tour de force" – Paul Moorcraft

Hardback; 228 x 155mm; 368 pages; 120 b/w & colour photographs;
map/sketches; 0 620 21573 9; 2ⁿᵈ Edition; Reprinted 1998, 1999, 2000

R185.00	£20.00	US$35.00	C$45.00	A$45.00	NZ$60.

ECHOES OF AN AFRICAN WAR
Chas Lotter

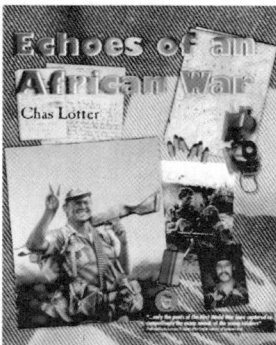

A photographic anthology by Africa's acclaimed soldier-poet. Coffee-table for with alternative pages of haunting poetry, mirrored by some stunning origin photography. Also a 150 leather-bound, gilded Limited Edition.

"...only the poets of the First World War have captured so compellingly the many moods of the young soldiers" – Professor Marcia Leveson, President of the English Academy of Southern Africa.

Hardback; 330 x 248mm; 208 pages; 650 colour photographs; 0 620 230

Standard: R295.00	£30.00	US$50.00	C$75.00	A$75.00	NZ$10
Limited: R995.00	£100.00	US$175.00	C$250.00	A$250.00	NZ$32

SURVIVAL COURSE

Chris Cocks

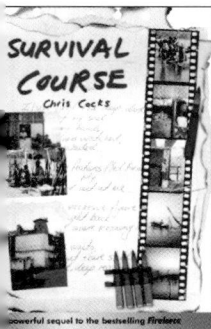

The sequel to the best-selling *Fireforce.* Chronicling the author's 15-month experience, up to Zimbabwean independence in 1980, as a stick-leader in the specialist PATU (Police Anti-Terrorist Unit), operating on Rhodesia's eastern border. Part Two of the book deals with the author's traumatic and harrowing transition to civilian life in post-war Zimbabwe.

Softback; 222 x 152mm; 244 pages; 40 b/w photographs,map; 0 620 24115 2

| R95.00 | £10.00 | US$17.50 | C$25.00 | A$25.00 | NZ$32.50 |

MAPOLISA – Some Reminiscences of a Rhodesian Policeman

David Craven

The author's memoirs of his service in the British South Africa Police (BSAP) 1948-69. Capturing a colonial era as "the winds of change" were blowing across Africa. A delightful account of an ordinary policeman simply getting on with his job.

"…a very readable story… which needed telling" – *Zimbabwe Independent*

Softback; 222 x 152mm; 216 pages; 66 b/w illustrations, map; 0 620 22522 X
Reprinted 2000

| R100.00 | £10.00 | US$17.50 | C$25.00 | A$25.00 | NZ$32.50 |

ONE COMMANDO – Rhodesia's Last Years, the Guerrilla War

Dick Gledhill

The author's fictionalized account of his service in the elite parachute battalion, One Commando, the Rhodesian Light Infantry, during the height of the guerrilla war. A cracker of a story; action-packed all the way. Well balanced and intriguing.

Softback; 178 x 111mm; 218 pages; 20 b/w photographs; 0 646 31036 4
RLI Publishing

| R100.00 | £10.00 | US$17.50 | C$25.00 | A$25.00 | NZ$32.50 |

CURRENTLY AVAILABLE

THE ELITE – The Story of the Rhodesian SAS

Barbara Cole

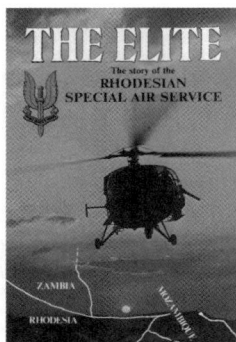

The best-selling account of "C" Squadron, the SAS during the Rhodesian bush w
of the 1970s. First published in 1985, this book is timeless in content and appea

"…possibly the most important book about the Rhodesian war from
military side" – Daily Dispatch

Softback ; 194 x 130mm; 461 pages; 56 b/w photographs, maps; 0 620 08517
Three Knights Publishing

R100.00	£10.00	US$17.50	C$25.00	A$25.00	NZ$32.5(

BUSH HORIZONS – The Story of Aviation in Southern Rhodesia 1896-19

Squadron Leader N.V. Phillips

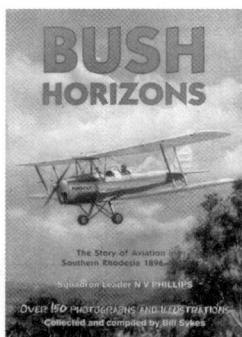

Edited by Group Captain Bill Sykes, Wing Commander Peter Cooke and Profess
Dick Christie. Packed with fascinating accounts of the development of flight in t
"early days" in Africa. A unique account that is a must for anyone remotely
interested in aviation.

Softback; 212 x 146mm; 204 pages; 146 b/w illustrations, maps; 0 797 4184
Air Forces Association; Reprinted 1999

R120.00	£15.00	US$25.00	C$35.00	A$35.00	NZ$45.(

FIRE, FLOOD AND ICE – Search and Rescue Missions
of the South African Air Force

Brigadier Dick Lord

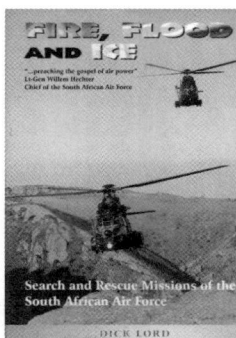

A compilation of South African search and rescue missions, both military and c
over the past decade. Foreword by Lieutenant-General Willem Hechter, Chief of
SAAF. Of heartwarming dedication and courage, these true stories will leave the
reader breathless.

Hardback; 228 x155mm; 280 pages; 90 b/w & colour photographs; 6 maps;
0 620 22901 2

R140.00	£15.00	US$25.00	C$35.00	A$35.00	NZ$45.0

PEN COCKPIT OVER AFRICA

tor Smith

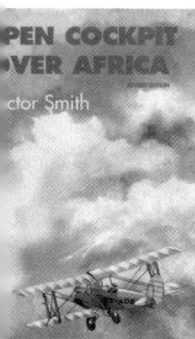

The intimate account by one of Africa's pioneering aviators, of what it was like to fly open-cockpit, single-engined aircraft the length and breadth of primitive Africa in the 1930s. A breathtaking and thrilling saga of aerial trail-blazing from London to the Cape and back. It is also of the author's experiences as Beaufighter pilot in the Balkan Air Force during World War II.

"...ranking with the best of Sir Francis Chichester's three books on his air pioneering travels" – Hammond Innes

Softback; 229 x 152mm; 196 pages; 58 b/w illustrations; maps, diagrams; 0 798 50773 X; Faircape Books

R120.00	£15.00	US$25.00	C$35.00	A$35.00	NZ$45.00

OW WE KEPT THE FLAG FLYING

ald Macdonald

Similar facsimile reprint of 1st Edition, (Ward, Lock & Co. Ltd., 1900). This enduring story of the siege of Ladysmith is the first in our series of Anglo-Boer War titles, commemorating the Anglo-Boer War Centenary 1999-2002. A classic in every sense, and as relevant today as a century ago.

Hardback; 213 x 137mm; 303 pages; 12 b/w illustrations; 0 620 23342 7 2nd Edition

R100.00	£15.00	US$25.00	C$35.00	A$35.00	NZ$45.00

LT! ACTION FRONT! – With Colonel Long at Colenso

rell Hall

The detailed account of the three batteries of the 4th Brigade Division, Royal Field Artillery (7th, 14th, and 66th), and the six "Long 12s" of the Royal Navy, which operated under the direct command of Colonel C.J. Long RHA, commanding the Artillery of the Natal Field Force, at the Battle of Colenso, on 15th December 1899. These three RFA batteries still serve today in the 26th Field Regiment, Royal Artillery, as now 16th, 17th and 159th respectively.

Hardback; 228 x 155mm; 208 pages; over 100 b/w photographs, diagrams, maps; 0 620 24112 8

R100.00	£15.00	US$25.00	C$35.00	A$35.00	NZ$45.00

CURRENTLY AVAILABLE

SOUTH AFRICAN WAR BOOKS – An Illustrated Bibliography

R.G. Hackett

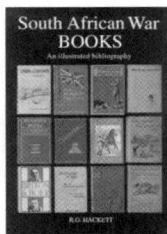

Definitive compilation of English language publications relating to the Anglo-Boer War 189ᴄ 1902. A masterpiece and already a collector's item, with only 1,200 copies printed.

*"**With meticulous regard for detail, this bibliography of contemporary books about the Boer War is a collector's must... a delightful insight into the mind the bibliophile...**" – Jim Mitchell, The Star*

Hardback; 316 x 222mm; 216 pages; Over 200 colour and b/w illustrations; 0 952 0039 P.G. de Lotz Military Bookseller

R850.00	£65.00	US$100.00	C$150.00	A$150.00	NZ$195.(

SAND IN THE WIND

Keith Meadows

Of wildlife and war, this haunting novel, drawn from factual events and set in the great Zam Valley encompasses the fading era of Rhodesia to the dawn of Zimbabwe. Evocatively captu the essence of wild Africa. Following the traditions of Robert Ruark.

*"**A land without animals is a dead land**" – Old Shangaan saying*

Softback; 220 x 148mm; 522 pages; 0 797 41785 0; Thorntree Press

R120.00	£15.00	US$25.00	C$35.00	A$35.00	NZ$45.0(

RUPERT FOTHERGILL – Bridging a Conservation Era

Keith Meadows

The full story of Operation Noah and its instigator, world-famous game warden Rupert Fothergill—the reluctant hero. The story of the famous animal rescue from the rising wate the Kariba Dam on the Zambezi River. Operation Noah was to become the cornerstone of Zimbabwe's progressive conservation policies. With beautiful sketches by renowned wildlife artist Ian Henderson.

Hardback; 214 x 150mm; 264 pages; 40 sepia photographs; 0 797 41608 0; Thorntree P.

R120.00	£15.00	US$25.00	C$35.00	A$35.00	NZ$45.(

WANKIE – The Story of a Great Game Reserve

Ted Davison

The enduring account of the birth and development of one of Africa's great game reserves– Hwange (Wankie) National Park in Zimbabwe—and the legendary ranger who started it all With the foreword by former prime minister, Ian Douglas Smith.

*"**There are some who can live without wild things, and some who cannot**" – A Leopold, A Sand County Almanac*

Hardback; 220 x 150mm; 276 pages; 87 sepia illustrations; Sketches, maps; 0 797 4187 3ʳᵈ Impression; Thorntree Press

R120.00	£15.00	US$25.00	C$35.00	A$35.00	NZ$45.(

CLONE BLUES

is Cocks

author's first novel after his best-selling nonfiction *Fireforce* and *Survival Course*. Set in present-day
babwe and Mozambique, still suffering from the hangovers of civil war – it is a story of love and tragedy,
nst the backdrop of political machinations and treachery. It successfully examines inter-racial relationships
attitudes and breathes hope into a troubled sub-continent, struggling with its history, its present and its
re.

ust; Softback; 222 x 152mm; 0 620 25438 6

NKASEKI – One day at a time

bur Titherington

n prisoner at the fall of Singapore, the author was to spend the rest of the war as a slave labourer in the
nese POW camp at Kinkaseki in Formosa (now Taiwan). A chilling exposé of brutality and cruelty. A true
of survival in the tradition of *Tenko* and *The Bridge on the River Kwai*.

ust; Softback; 222 x 152 mm; illustrated; 2nd Edition; 0 620 25441 6

IE MANY HOUSES OF EXILE

bard Jurgens

cinating autobiographical account of the author's experiences as an ANC exile. From his conscription into
outh African army, to ANC recruitment whilst studying philosophy at Wits University – to life in the ANC
ps in Zambia, Tanzania and Zimbabwe – and finally to 8 years exile in Holland. Richard Jurgens is the new
e of South African literature.

ust; Softback; 222 x 152mm; 0 620 25440 8

IE REGIMENT – A History and the Uniforms of the
tish South Africa Police

k Hamley

nning coffee-table pictorial production, with the author's own vivid water-colour plates included. Traces
evelopment of this fine police force from the 1890s to 1980. Also a Special leather-bound Edition.

ember; Softback; illustrated; 2nd Edition; 0 620 25394 0

PRIDE OF EAGLES – The Definitive History of the
odesian Air Force 1920-80

l Salt

a the arrival of the *Silver Queen* in 1920, through the "Rhodesia squadrons" of World War 2, to the
tion of hostilities after the Rhodesian bush war in 1980, the author has spent over 30 years compiling this
prehensive account of this small, but professional and effective air force. Officially endorsed by the Air
Associations of Zimbabwe, this book will be prized by lovers of Africana and aviation buffs worldwide. Also
ited Edition of 75 copies.

mber; Hardback; illustrated; maps/diagrams; 0 620 23759 7

COVOS-DAY BOOKS

P. O. Box 6996
Weltevredenpark, 1715
South Africa

tel +2711-475 0922
fax +2711-475 8974
email: covos@global.co.za
website at: www.mazoe.com

UK/Europe Sales and Distribution
VERULAM PUBLISHING

152a Park Street Lane, Park Street
St Albans, Herts AL2 2AU
tel: +44-1727-872 770
fax +44-1727-873 866
email: verulampub@compuserve.com

ЖDER FORM

Yes, I would like to order

ιe	Quantity	Currency	Total
Total Postage			
Total Order			

Address

code .... Country

.... (include country/area code)

.... (include country/area code)

ЛENT OPTION

I enclose a cheque/bank draft for the total value of the order

Please charge the amount of .... to my Visa/Master card

Card no

Expiry date .... Last 3 digits on reverse of card

Signature .... Date

your order and payment to:

Day Books
ox 6996, Weltevredenpark
South Africa

or fax/email your order and credit card details to:
fax +2711-475 8974
email: covos@global.co.za

ιay also choose to order via our website at **www.mazoe.com**

ge rates per one book

ιnation	South Africa	UK; Europe	USA; Asia; S.America	Canada	Australia	New Zealand
ιce Mail	R25.00	£8.50	$15.00	C$20.00	A$20.00	NZ$25.00
ail	n/a	£14.50	$25.00	C$35.00	A$35.00	NZ$45.00

ιtes include postage, packaging and insurance
ease select either Surface Mail (4-8 weeks delivery outside of RSA) or Airmail (7-10 days delivery) and add the total
& P charges to your order
ιr Limited and Special Editions, please double the P & P rates
r orders of 3 books or more, please deduct 25% off the total P & P costs